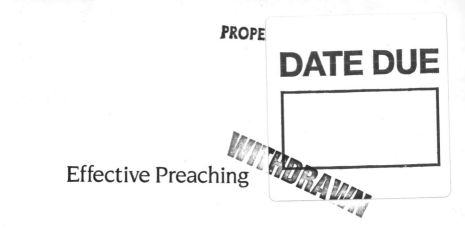

PROPE

DATE DUE

Effective Preaching

D0028980

Effective Preaching

A Manual
for Students
and Pastors

Deane A. Kemper

The Westminster Press
Philadelphia

Scripture quotations from the Revised Standard Version of the Bible are copyrighted 1946, 1952, © 1971, 1973 by the Division of Christian Education of the National Council of the Churches of Christ in the U.S.A. and are used by permission.

The Schramm model of communication in chapter 1 is reprinted by permission of the University of Illinois Press from W. Schramm, "How Communication Works," in W. Schramm, ed., *The Process and Effects of Mass Communication* (Urbana, IL: University of Illinois Press, 1955), p. 6.

The quotation by Vincent Drayne in chapter 5 is reprinted with permission from "How to Lose an Audience" in the September 1967 issue of the *Public Relations Journal,* Copyright 1967.

Book design by Gene Harris

First edition

Published by The Westminster Press®
Philadelphia, Pennsylvania

PRINTED IN THE UNITED STATES OF AMERICA
9 8 7 6 5 4 3 2 1

Library of Congress Cataloging in Publication Data

Kemper, Deane A. (Deane Alwyn), 1940–
   Effective preaching.

   Bibliography: p.
   Includes index.
   1. Preaching. I. Title.
BV4211.2.K395 1985   251   84-20880
ISBN 0-664-24595-1 (pbk.)

To Rachel and Susanna

My sharpest listeners
and kindest critics

Contents

Preface

In Calvin's Geneva there lived a citizen who could well be the patron saint of countless lay people throughout the history of the church. When the city elders demanded that this Monsieur Belard appear before them to tell why he refused to attend divine services and hear the Word of God, he replied that he was more than willing to hear the Word of God, but not those preachers!

The complaint of the humble Genevan church member has been heard in our own generation as we experience a renewed emphasis on the Word in Christian preaching. The concept of the biblical sermon stems from a healthy reaction to a brace of competing homiletical philosophies of the modernist-fundamentalist controversy of the 1920s and 1930s: the expository mode, generally that of the fundamentalists, and the topical approach, favored mainly by the modernists. The rise of neo-orthodoxy not only established a theological center between the poles but also brought a fresh appreciation of the central place of the Bible in preaching. The earlier, expository sermon, which was often little more than a thinly disguised lecture on a biblical text, and the topical sermon, which could be a discourse on a contemporary concern or event with scant biblical support, gave way to the biblical sermon, in which a Scripture text was exegeted and proclaimed to address a life situation. The homiletical literature of today is replete with titles on biblical preaching from the pens of authors representing both the theological left and the right.

It is the assumption of this book that sound exegesis is a prerequisite to sound sermons. Good exegetical material does not always result in effective preaching, however, if the preacher is unable to incorporate the biblical data into a comprehensive, comprehensible, and stimulating sermonic whole. Simply stated, performing a thorough, faithful, and cogent exegetical study of a biblical text is foundational to good preaching, and this effort represents about one third of the required labor for a worthwhile sermon. Working with that exegetical material through the organization, manuscript, and delivery stages constitutes the remaining two thirds of the job. It is this two thirds of the preacher's task, from exegesis through delivery, that is the focus of this volume.

There are probably as many methods of sermonizing as there are preachers, and for one preacher to attempt to employ another's working methodology is about as practical as wearing someone else's shoes. This presentation is in no way to be construed as the only or even the preferred approach to the homiletical craft—and there will be reminders of this disclaimer from time to time in the pages that follow. By precept and example, this book sets out a working pattern for preparing and delivering sermons. The reader is encouraged not to adopt this method wholesale but to interact with it, retaining what is valuable and appropriate, modifying what is worth keeping with some change, and rejecting what is unsuited to the preacher's setting, tradition, and personality.

Not long ago, at the close of the school year, an Oriental student came to express thanks for my first course in preaching, which he had just completed. "I very much appreciated your course and learned a lot about preaching, Dr. Kemper," he said with a gracious smile, "but I had to reject about eighty percent of what you had to say." This seemed to be a rather unusual compliment until he went on to explain himself. "If I went home and preached in Chinese the way you taught us in class, the people wouldn't stand for it." He then described several critical differences between preaching as it is practiced in his homeland and preaching as we know it in North America.

Even on our continent, however, preaching is not a monolithic institution. The sermon preached on Sunday morning in the downtown Pentecostal storefront church will differ considerably from the bishop's homily delivered in the Roman Catholic cathedral a few blocks away. There may be contrasts within the same denomination, as in the message delivered by the pastor of a university Methodist church as opposed to his or her colleague in a rural parish fifteen miles away.

For those who preach in whatever circumstances, this book is intended to be a popular and readable treatment of its subject. Although there is biblical, theological, rhetorical, and homiletical research underlying the themes presented, the emphasis is on the practical, and documentation has been kept to a minimum. It is my hope that students and pastors from a variety of traditions and settings will find this book helpful in proclaiming the gospel message with sincerity, simplicity, and power.

D.A.K.

Nantucket Island

Acknowledgments

There are many good people to whom I owe much gratitude for their part in this study. Some of them made my work easier, a few made it more difficult, all made it better. The shortcomings in these pages are mine alone.

My special thanks is extended to Ann Madsen Dailey and my daughter, Rachel, who read early drafts of each chapter; to Bob Briggs, who provided a word processor; to homiletical colleagues Don Wardlaw of McCormick Theological Seminary and Robert Schaper of Fuller Theological Seminary, who gave excellent advice and counsel; to the trustees of Gordon-Conwell Theological Seminary, who granted a sabbatical year for research and writing; to Gwyn Walters, Samuel Hogan, and Patricia Budd Kepler, who most capably carried my teaching load during that year; to my students, who have taught me at least as much as I have taught them; and to faithful secretaries Nancy Allen and Barbara DeNike, who read my scratchings and accommodated countless changes in typing the final manuscript—all without complaint. (Well, almost without complaint.)

Thank you each and every one.

1
Defining the Task

Preaching has been at the heart of the Christian tradition from the beginning. John the Baptist came preaching, and Jesus after him, both standing as the culmination of a long line of Old Testament prophets. After Pentecost, the apostles, in obedience to the Word and example of the risen Christ, preached the gospel of the Kingdom to the Mediterranean world. As the church grew, each succeeding generation set apart certain members for the office of ordained ministry who went into the world proclaiming the Christian message. We who preach today are the contemporary practitioners of an ancient and honorable calling.

Despite the pervasive practice of the homiletical craft throughout the history of Christianity, those who preach continue to struggle to define precisely what the sermon is. Seminarians and beginning preachers pose a variety of questions: Must a sermon always have a biblical text? How does (or should) a lecture by a New Testament scholar on 1 Corinthians 6:12–20 differ from a pastor's sermon on the same passage? Could an article in *The Christian Century, Sojourners,* or *Christianity Today* be properly identified as a sermon?

In teaching homiletics courses, I work from a traditional definition of preaching of my own design:

Preaching: the proclamation by the spoken word of the Incarnate
Word as revealed in the written word in such a manner as to initiate
Christian commitment, accentuate Christian experience, create
Christian attitudes, and motivate Christian action.

As an academic definition, this contribution touches most
bases: preaching is oral communication of the Christ-event as
recorded in the Bible with specific behavioral objectives: evangelism, belief reinforcement, attitude creation, and motivation. It
is, however, a definition that focuses on the *intent* of the sermon
but reveals little or nothing of the *content.*

Components of the Sermon

A century ago, in his famous Lyman Beecher Lectures at
Yale, Phillips Brooks first stated his definition of preaching that
to this day finds its way into nearly every book printed on the
subject:

> What, then, is preaching, of which we are to speak? It is not hard
> to find a definition. Preaching is the communication of truth by man
> to men. It has in it two essential elements, truth and personality.
> Neither of these can it spare. . . . Preaching is the bringing of truth
> through personality.
>
> (*Lectures on Preaching,* p. 5)

George Sweazey of Princeton Theological Seminary is one of
the few with the temerity to tamper with Brooks's definition,
expanding it to read "truth through personality *in the midst of
personalities*" (Sweazey, p. 5; his emphasis). This significant
addition brings us closer to a viable statement of the nature of
the sermon, for a complete dissection of the finished product
of the preacher's craft reveals not two but three essential components: the Word (or truth, in Brooks's definition), the
human situation, and the preacher's personality. In the small
arena where the preacher proclaims the Word of God to the
human situation through the filter of his or her own personality, the sermon has its life and being. (See Figure 1.)

The area of overlap is small, for in any single sermon the
preacher addresses not the whole of human need but only a

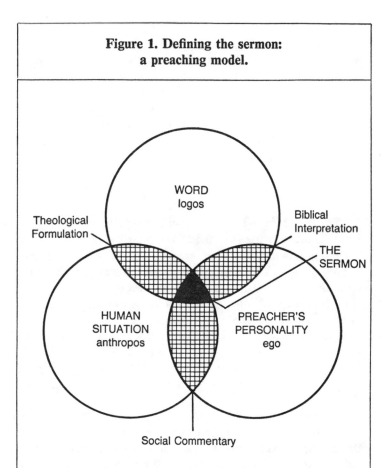

**Figure 1. Defining the sermon:
a preaching model.**

WORD
logos

Theological
Formulation

Biblical
Interpretation

THE
SERMON

HUMAN
SITUATION
anthropos

PREACHER'S
PERSONALITY
ego

Social Commentary

Figure 1. *Defining the sermon: a preaching model.* The sermon is an address from the Word of God to the human situation through the filter of the preacher's personality. It is at once theological, sociological, and psychological in nature. In addition to the three components of Word (logos), Humanity (anthropos), and Personality (ego), the preacher, in preparing the sermon, engages in the three areas of overlap: theological formulation, social commentary, and biblical interpretation.

single issue or, even more likely, one facet of a single issue. The preacher does not attempt to elucidate the whole of the Word, only a small portion. No preacher would be willing or able to disclose an entire personality in that one sermon, only that part of the personality which interacts with the segment of the human situation being addressed and the portion of the Word chosen as text. Thus, the area where the three components touch each other is tiny indeed.

The Word

"The Word [*logos*] became flesh and dwelt among us" (John 1:14), and the written record of the Word is contained in the Scriptures. As Jesus called apostles to himself and sent them out to bear witness to what they had learned and experienced in life with him, so the preachers in each succeeding generation of the church have proclaimed the Christ known by faith as revealed in the pages of the Bible.

In considering the *logos*—"word"—as both incarnate and inscribed, it is theoretically possible to drive a wedge between Christ and the Bible and argue that the sermon may indeed proclaim the Word of God without the benefit of a scriptural text.

While such preaching may be possible, it is at best a hazardous undertaking. The Bible is a source of protection both for those who deliver sermons and for those who hear them. A definite biblical text sets limits for the sermon, first by stimulating the imagination of the preacher and then by holding that imagination in check. The preacher is not likely to wander too far afield if the sermon continually returns to a biblical foundation. A specific biblical passage also serves to root the sermon in historic revelation. It is the Scriptures, and not we ourselves, that bear witness to God's mighty acts of redemption. A sermon that faithfully expounds the written Word will remain true to God's revealing of himself in history.

The Human Situation

While the sermon, properly conceived, is biblically based, it is not biblically directed. That is to say, the sermon does not (or should not) focus on the biblical text but uses that text to focus attention on a particular human problem or question. There is more than the mere interchange of prepositions in the distinction that the preacher preaches *from* a text, not *on* a text. The Old Testament scholar may lecture *on* Isaiah 40 with the intent of presenting a thorough and cogent exegesis of the passage that will add to the amount of knowledge of the Old Testament held by those who hear the presentation. The preacher will exegete the passage but will then preach *from* Isaiah 40 *to* the life situation of those assembled to hear the proclamation of the Word. To be sure, there is an educational dimension to preaching, and we would wish those hearing the sermon to know more of the prophecy of Isaiah at the close of the message than at the beginning, but the primary intent of the sermon is to address a specific issue or problem, not to convey information.

Karl Barth applied Paul Tillich's phrase "awareness of the present moment" to the life setting of preaching. "What demands does the contemporary situation make on the preacher and his congregation?" asked Barth. "Together they are sharing an historical experience" (*Prayer and Preaching,* p. 97). It is this shared sense of history that is at the heart of preaching. Indeed, it is its *raison d'être,* for it is in the act of preaching that God addresses his Word to his people in their anxiety and hope, failure and potential, despair and joy, grief and celebration.

The Preacher's Personality

There is perhaps no concept more difficult for beginning preachers to understand than the role of personality in preaching. While a few naturally gregarious pulpiteers need to be restrained from preaching in a manner that reveals more of the minister than the message, most young preachers find their early sermonic efforts to be genuinely stressful occasions. The very real human emotions of self-consciousness and stage fright are operative here, but so too is the healthy conviction of many that preaching is God's work and is not to be done in human strength alone. Even when conceding that some intrusion of the personality is inevitable in matters of structure, word choice, and manner of speech, there are a good many preachers who consciously attempt to conceal their personalities behind the sermon as a theological event. As often as not, the finished product in manuscript form is an uncertain essay reading suspiciously like a journal article by an insecure academician writing in dread of contradiction. In delivery, a deliberately subdued manner may be affected so as not to distract from the verbal message. (Such a preacher will often argue that the content of the sermon is "real" while the delivery, if not "unreal," is certainly "less real.") The tedium that results in either case is rooted in the failure of the preacher to understand that the preaching of the gospel has been instituted by our Lord so that the personality of the proclaimer is an integral part of the act itself.

Marshall McLuhan, in his book *Understanding Media*, depicted technological advances as extensions of the human body. Thus, the wheel is an extension of the foot, the book is an extension of the eye, clothing is an extension of the skin, and electronic circuitry is an extension of the central nervous system. Following McLuhan homiletically, it could be argued that the sermon is an extension of the soul, for it is clearly the divine intent that the Word of God be communicated from person to person. In fact, one of the most unfortunate and inappropriate labels ever to be employed within the Christian tradition is that of the "social gospel." It is, of course, a tautology. The gospel is by its very nature and definition social and is clearly described as such in Scripture, for not only did Jesus accomplish the task of preaching the Kingdom by sending out apostles to share the message in word and deed in the cities and towns of Israel, but Paul asked rhetorically:

> But how are men to call upon him in whom they have not believed?
> And how are they to believe in him of whom they have never heard?
> And how are they to hear without a preacher?
>
> (Romans 10:14)

The meaning of the word "gospel" is, of course, "good news." By definition, news is a message conveyed by a source who has knowledge to a receiver who does not. The truth of the Christian message is both propositional and experiential. While propositional knowledge may be adequately conveyed by the printed page or the electronic media, the sharing of experience is rendered difficult if not impossible when removed from the personal setting. The preaching of the gospel, therefore, is a social institution conjoining the personality of the one who preaches with the personalities of those who hear.

Processes of the Sermon

In addition to the center area, where all three components meet to produce the sermon, the model also depicts three shaded regions created by the overlapping of two components (see Figure 1). While these areas do not represent the sermon per se, they do indicate traditional disciplines in the theological enterprise, as well as labor performed by the preacher in process of preparing and delivering sermons. These areas of activity bear the labels Theological Formulation, Social Commentary, and Biblical Interpretation.

Theological Formulation

The task of delineating theological doctrine is commonly assumed to be the work of the professional theologian. Yet both the preacher and the systematic theologian go about their work in constant contact with both "word" and "situation." The difference between the two labors is largely one of scope. The theologian considers the entire human predicament and the whole of God's revelation and, over a period of years, develops a schematic representation of humanity's relationship to God. The preacher isolates one particle of the human predicament and studies one portion of the Word and each week brings the resulting message to a specific congregation. Over a period of years, the efforts of the preacher will stand no less than those of the theologian as a systematic theology, but no one sermon will represent the entire scheme. Instead, each sermon will be directed to one specific, concrete situation.

Often the task of theological formulation is performed corporately, as in the drafting and adoption of credal statements. Such efforts represent the church's response to the forces of society, culture, science, technology, or history bringing pressure to bear on the Christian community. It is significant that the creed is not the statement of a person, or even persons, but the corporate confession of the church. In addressing the world confessionally, the church brings the Word to the human situation, but the factor of personality is deliberately excluded: the creed belongs to the church.

The same is true of the liturgy, which is the corporate expression of the people of faith in worship. The sermon, by way of contrast, is the personal expression of the preacher. The minister submits both life and ministry to the confessional stand of the church in taking ordination vows, and the minister by call of the congregation submits to the liturgical tradition of the church as well. The sermon at its very heart, however, contains the dimension of personality not shared with creed or liturgy, and in assuming the office of preacher, the man or woman of God proclaims the divine Word personally as well as corporately.

Social Commentary

Unlike the publishing of theology, the propagation of social commentary is not a uniquely religious activity. James Reston does it, as does William F. Buckley. George Will, Mort Sahl, Mary McGrory, and Phyllis Schlafly are all social critics in the secular sphere. Some media outlets are devoted almost entirely to social analysis: *The Nation, The New Republic, National Review,* and, on television, "Saturday Night Live" and "60 Minutes." Of more immediate concern for our purposes is religious social commentary of the sort available in the pages of *Christianity and Crisis, Commonweal,* and the *Reformed Journal,* to name a few publications, or expressed by such individuals as

Rosemary Ruether, Andrew Greeley, John Fry, Letha Scanzoni, Martin Marty, and Franky Schaeffer.

Like the sermon and unlike the creed, the work of the religious social critic is a personal statement. Even though many if not most of the generally read writers of Christian social criticism are ordained ministers, there remain differences in approach, if not intent, between the preacher and the social commentator. The preacher speaks to a problem or issue in either the religious or secular sphere from a distinct portion of the Word. The social critic also addresses problems and issues in the religious and secular realms, but from a more general biblical orientation. To be sure, incisive social commentary will make use of relevant biblical texts, but the issues considered are far too vast and complex to employ the economical format of the sermon. If a dangerous generalization may be permitted, all sermons are Christian social commentary, but not all Christian social commentary is sermonic. That is, in the very act of opening the Scriptures and addressing the Word to a congregation, the preacher is commenting on the social order. The social critic, meanwhile, paints his or her canvas in much broader strokes, both in analysis of society and in biblical application.

The skilled preacher is inevitably an astute observer of human behavior and brings to the sermon both personal judgments of the social order and the comments of professionals in the field. In preparing the sermon, however, the preacher will in almost every case take the broad social judgment of the critic and apply it to a restricted local situation. For example, the parish minister will absorb the comments of Christian social thinkers on the issue of poverty but in taking the pulpit will apply that thinking to specific cases of economic imbalance in the immediate community.

Biblical Interpretation

It could be argued that biblical scholars are the bottom link in the environmental food chain of the church. Preachers, educators, theologians, and ethicists all consume the work of the exegetes as an energy source for their own disciplines. Or, to switch the metaphor from the biological to the industrial, Old and New Testament researchers are the miners bringing the raw materials to the surface for their colleagues in other fields to fashion into finished products. (Often those working outside the biblical fields grumble over the quality of the data provided, and just as often the biblical scholars complain about the violence done to their findings; but this is a tension as old as theological scholarship.)

The fruits of biblical research are passed on to the theologians to arrange into a consistent system of belief, and to the preachers to apply to the concerns of the contemporary church. The preacher stands without apology as the popularizer of theological research—the link between the people in the pew and the scholar in the library. In the preparation of sermons, the preacher, working with a restricted topic and a brief text, has more in common with the biblical theologian than the dogmatic theologian. Throughout the history of the church, in fact, the separation of interpretation and proclamation has been less than absolute. In the preaching of John Chrysostom, there was no clear line between sermon and commentary—and his practice reflected that of the ancient church. In more recent times, the heart of John Wesley was strangely warmed by reading Luther's introduction to his Commentary on Romans, and Karl Barth's *Römerbrief* spoke to an entire generation.

The significant differences between the preacher and the interpreter lie not so much in approach to the text as in what is done with the text. As stated previously, the primary concern of the biblical scholar is the meaning of the text at the time of writing, while the concern of the preacher is the application of the text to the contemporary situation. Biblical commentators are not isolated from current concerns (witness the mountain of exegetical data recently produced on issues relating to women in the Scriptures), but they must take care not to approach the Bible with a socially determined agenda.

There remains an important factor of time dividing commentary from homily. Good biblical interpretation, based on thorough language study and conducted according to sound hermeneutical procedures, may be written, published, circulated, and used profitably for hundreds of years. A sermon, even when set down in manuscript form, is oral discourse designed for the ear to hear at a precise moment of time and in a certain place. Even though a sermon may be printed and circulated so that it commands a greater reading than its original hearing (as more people have read Shakespeare's plays than seen them staged), the work of the preacher, as that of the bard, is oral communication first and literature second. Good biblical interpretation is produced on the printed page and will remain useful for a century or more. Good preaching is spoken in acoustic space and need only be useful in the present moment.

The human and divine nature of the sermon was rightly assessed by Karl Barth: "Preaching is a human activity and thus stained with sin, but it is also both commanded and blest by God and, therefore, has a promise attached to it" (*Prayer and Preaching*, p. 87). The dual presence of humanity and divinity in preaching is the logical conclusion of the process in which God has sought to communicate his love to humankind. In the frailty of human form the *logos* came to earth. In the weakness of a human book the *logos* has been revealed to succeeding generations. In the foolishness of a human act the *logos* is proclaimed to the world.

2
Determining the Subject

Any single product of human creativity, be it sermon, sonnet, novel, symphony, painting, sculpture, or essay, begins with a single idea. Some artistic people have the luxury of virtually unlimited time: a symphony, drama, or novel may be the fruit of months or years of labor. Even the student working in the time constraints of academia has the better part of a term to formulate the idea for a paper and then write and submit the finished product for a grade.

The parish pastor is no less a creative person than the artist. Unlike the writer, composer, or painter, however, or even unlike the student, the minister does not have months, years, or terms to discover, formulate, and nurture a creative seed. The hour of worship comes at the same time each week, and Sunday in and Sunday out, year after year, it is the good pastor's responsibility to feed the flock. Coming up with a sermon that is worth hearing every week during a lifetime of ministry is a considerable task, but there is no reason why it must be burdensome. Indeed, the preacher who is willing to read, observe, listen, and learn may have the happy experience of choosing sermon topics from many suitable subjects rather than searching desperately for a message to fill the Sunday morning void.

The Essential Question

In beginning the work of preaching, it is good to keep in mind a foundational question that establishes the task and its six components: Why should this *congregation* in this *church* on this *occasion* listen to this *preacher* deliver this *sermon* from this *text?*

The question is posed not from the perspective of those who preach sermons but from the perspective of those who hear them, and it asks that we who open the Scriptures and address the Christian community justify our activity. Why should the good lay people in First Church sit silently and dutifully in their pews, giving at least relatively undivided attention, while the pastor has his or her say? It is hardly an unfair question, for even in a congregation of 200 worshipers the service of worship absorbs 200 person-hours of time, and the largest single unit of that 200 hours is the sermon.

A consideration of the six constituent parts of the question gives a sense of the complexity of the preaching situation.

1. *The congregation:* Those who hear and are joined together in the preaching moment—members and nonmembers, women and men, old and young, believers and nonbelievers alike.

2. *The church:* A complex structure embracing not only the congregation gathered in the sanctuary but also the entire local parish. Included as well is the denominational affiliation and the larger theological/ecclesiastical tradition: Roman Catholic, Reformed, Anabaptist, Lutheran, Pentecostal, Fundamentalist. In many churches there may be a specific ethnic component: Scandinavian Lutheran, Black Baptist, Dutch Reformed, French Roman Catholic, New England Yankee Congregationalist.

3. *The occasion:* A day or season of the Christian year—Advent, Christmas, Epiphany, Lent, Easter, Pentecost, Trinity; a day of the civil calendar—New Year's Day, Independence Day, Thanksgiving; an important occasion or anniversary in the life of the local church; a significant denominational day or program; a time of awareness of a

particular issue in the community, the nation, or the world.

4. *The preacher:* The person who addresses the congregation, who in all cases is a fellow struggler in the Christian life with those who listen; usually the pastor of the congregation but sometimes a guest unknown to the people, such as a visitor from a denominational or community ministry or even a theological student, a member of the church who is home from seminary on vacation.

5. *The sermon:* The discourse based on Scripture prepared and delivered by the preacher for the benefit of the congregation.

6. *The text:* The specific lesson(s) from the Bible chosen by the preacher to be the biblical foundation of the sermon.

Understanding the Process of Sermonic Communication

The goals of preaching as indicated in the definition in chapter 1 are evangelism, faith development, attitude creation, and motivation to Christian living. Obviously, no one sermon can accomplish all these purposes (even though we hear some that struggle mightily in the attempt). It is a wise preacher who determines the purpose of the sermon from the outset and targets specific people within the congregation as primary recipients of the message. An overview of the strategy of preaching may be seen in the model developed by Wilbur L. Schramm (Figure 2).

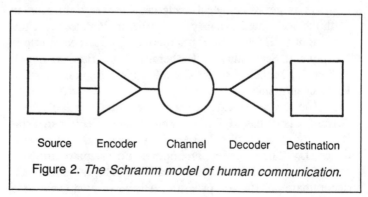

Source   Encoder   Channel   Decoder   Destination

Figure 2. *The Schramm model of human communication.*

If you read from left to right, the model shows the process of human communication, beginning with the source of an idea, the encoding of that idea into language or symbol, the presentation of the idea through channels that are perceived by the senses, the decoding of the message by those who perceive it, and the reception of the message by those whom it is intended to reach. The model presents in simple linear fashion what may be an extremely complex process.

Personal Conversation

A simple example is a conversation involving two people on a park bench. Ann, seated on the east end, is both *source* and *encoder* as she expresses her ideas through the *channel* of the spoken word to Bob on the west end, who is both *decoder* and *destination*. When Bob responds, the roles are reversed; he becomes *source* and *encoder,* Ann the *decoder* and *destination*. Any number of complicating factors could be introduced, but the two-person conversation is the simplest application of the model.

Mass Media

A more complex example is the television advertising of an expensive product such as the Mercedes-Benz automobile. In North America, television is a popular medium which only the poorest households are unable to afford. Yet in advertising its cars, Mercedes seeks to reach only that small percentage of the populace with sufficient income to pay $25,000 or more for a car. Accordingly, the company sponsors special programs, golf tournaments, and newscasts that are likely to attract well-educated, affluent, middle-aged viewers. When applied to our model, Mercedes-Benz is the *source* of communication, its advertising agency the *encoder,* television is the *channel,* the mass audience watching the sponsored program the *decoder,* and those in high-income brackets desiring an expensive car the *destination*. While the company reaps some benefits in that portion of the audience that cannot afford its automobiles by enhancing the prestige of the Mercedes name, the fact remains that Mercedes-Benz spends millions of dollars on television advertising (not to mention newspapers, magazines, and billboards) knowing that fewer than 3 percent of those who decode the ads can ever afford to buy the product.

Sermonic Communication

In the isolation of a target destination, the sermon lies somewhere between the personal conversation and the media advertising campaign in complexity. Bob and Ann, whom we left on the park bench, are perfectly content to communicate with each other with no secondary audience listening in—particularly if that park bench is on a riverbank bathed in moonlight on a balmy June evening. The Mercedes commercials, however, are actually enhanced by the mass secondary audience aspiring to own what is difficult to attain and attributing status to the product and those who drive it.

The sermon lacks the intimacy of Ann and Bob on the bench, but it shares the vitality of the live setting in which the one who speaks and those who hear are joined in physical proximity. As mass communication, the sermon, like the commercial, is a message spoken by a single voice (the preacher) to a large, heterogeneous receiver (the congregation). In preaching, in relation to the Schramm model, the Bible is the *source* of the message, the preacher is the *encoder*, the spoken word is the *channel*, the congregation is the *decoder*, and the smaller body within the congregation with a special need to hear and act on the message is the *destination*.

The principle of the *destination* within the *decoder* is not at all difficult to comprehend when put in typical preaching contexts. The evangelist preaches a gospel sermon from John 3:16 —"God so loved the world that he gave his only Son, that whoever believes in him should not perish but have eternal life" —with the goal of having those outside the Christian faith respond to an invitation. The entire congregation hears and decodes the message. The great majority of these hearers are good and loyal church folk who benefit from a retelling of the gospel but feel no need to answer the evangelist's call. The *destination* of the sermon, and those from whom the preacher does seek a direct response, is that smaller group within the larger—those who have never made a first commitment of faith.

The pastor of First Church in making the rounds of the parish in midwinter senses a spirit of depression in several members. The pastor takes to the study and works up a sermon from Philippians 1:19–26, in which Paul writes from prison about maintaining an attitude of rejoicing and placing his confidence in the prayers of the faithful and the spirit of Christ in achieving his deliverance. When the pastor takes to the pulpit, the entire congregation decodes the message. As all Christians endure gloomy periods of anxiety, pessimism, and doubt at some time in their pilgrimage of faith, there is a general application that is of value for all hearers. The primary target of the preacher, however, is that smaller number of people in the sanctuary who are struggling with despair right now. For this group (both those who are known to the pastor and those who are not), the sermon has immediate relevance; for those who have a family member or close friend in a similar state, the relevance is only slightly less; for Christians who have experienced such a time in their lives or who will in the future, the sermon will still have value.

Isolating Text and Subject

The presence of a text from the Bible does not render a sermon biblical, and its absence does not make it unbiblical. Martin Luther argued that the sermon could indeed be faithful to the Bible without the benefit of a specific text, and most of us learned long ago to our sorrow that just because a preacher opens the Bible and reads a lesson there is no guarantee that the message which follows will have anything to do with the text or even be biblical. Even the long-standing practice of peppering the sermon with "the Bible says" and quoting verses in the manner of a revivalist may produce a sermon that is less than the sum of its biblical parts.

The case has been argued in the previous chapter for the essential practice of basing the sermon on a biblical text. In most branches of the Christian tradition there is a de facto relationship between Scripture readings and sermons: the Bible is read aloud in worship and the sermon is based on the reading. There has been long debate, however, as to the proper starting point for the sermon. One school of thought contends that the sermonic process must always start with a biblical text, and from that portion of Holy Writ the preacher may generate a subject and prepare the sermon. Over against this view is the conviction of those who see the origins of the sermon in the congregation: the pastor considers the flock and its needs and then turns to the Bible for a text that supports the subject of the sermon. The usual debate (greatly oversimplified) between the two points of view says, on one side, that preaching that begins anywhere other than the Bible is likely to be excessively subjective. As a result, the congregation is more likely to hear the word of the pastor than the Word of God. From the other side comes the rejoinder that always beginning in the Bible places the preacher in a textual straitjacket that does not permit the addressing of sharp, specific, immediate concerns in the local church.

The argument is incomplete on both sides. For those who begin in the Bible, the very choice of the text for the sermon is a subjective act, and even those who preach from lessons for the day in a lectionary may opt to preach from one of the three lessons, two of the three, or all three. Selectivity also influences those who preach through a book or portion of the Bible; the choice of the Scripture reading that will be the basis of their series of sermons is a subjective choice. On the other side, the relational preachers who look first to the life of the people may find themselves restricted by the very freedom they seek. For instance, a preaching program that jumps from issue to issue may be imperiled by the tyranny of the immediate. A hopscotch approach to the Bible may result in the failure of lay people to gain a systematic knowledge of the Word that would enable them to think biblically and apply the teaching of the Bible in life situations.

When all is said and done, however, it is not the starting point but the finishing point that makes a sermon biblical. A National Basketball Association coach has said, "I don't have a starting five. I have a finishing five." The point made by the coach is that the lineup on the floor in the fourth quarter with the game on the line is more important than the five players taking their positions at the opening tap-off when there are no points on the scoreboard. Homiletically, it is where the sermon ends, what it teaches of the Bible, how it addresses the life of the congregation, and the demands it makes of God's people that renders it biblical—and the starting point matters much less. Such preaching may have its genesis in any or all of the six components of preaching from our essential question.

The Congregation

In the course of pastoral duties, a preacher will find a multitude of sermon subjects arising from ordinary settings: the hospital visit to a terminally ill cancer patient, the church school committee meeting, the prebaptismal conference with parents of a newborn baby, the counseling session with the wife of an alcoholic husband, the youth group meeting in which the young people openly express their anxiety about nuclear war. Harry Emerson Fosdick often drew sermon subjects from his counseling ministry, assuming that for every person who came to him with a particular problem there were ten or a dozen more in the parish struggling with the same difficulty. While counseling is a fruitful source of sermon material, an obvious word of caution is in order. The pastor must be sufficiently general and nonspecific so as to safeguard confidences.

The Church (Denomination)

Denominations generate many resources for use in parish ministry. Traditionally, pastors grumble about the mail from church headquarters, grousing about administrators with spare computer time and an idle printing press who believe that parish pastors have nothing better to do than implement yet another new program. In the midst of all the verbiage, however, there are some gems that can and should find their way into sermons, such as materials and programs designed to involve the local church in stewardship, evangelism, community work, missions, and peacemaking. Many denominations distribute program calendars that are valuable aids in planning church schedules, worship emphases, and preaching topics months in advance. Special bulletins, posters, and other materials may be ordered to supplement and enrich the preaching and worship life of the parish.

The Occasion

No two preaching events are precisely alike. The variables approach infinity. As the gospel is preached in the context of the Christian tradition, the initial consideration should be the day or season of the church year. There are days and events in the civil calendar that present good sermon opportunities as well, although some care must be exercised to avoid a secularization of the pulpit. In addition, there are recurring events, controversies, and issues in the life of the congregation, community, nation, and world that need to be put in theological context from the pulpit. Typical examples could be the well-publicized operations of a religious cult in the local area, a state council of churches legal-aid program for migrant farm workers, an international crisis that raises anxiety in church families whose sons face draft registration, or a recent criminal execution creating a controversy in which prominent Christians are quoted in the media for and against capital punishment—with both sides using the Bible to support their cases.

The Preacher

Many powerful sermons emerge from deep within the soul of the pastor. The preacher may reveal a particular religious experience or a longer spiritual journey as an encouragement for the congregation. Some prudence is required, however, for a congregation that hears too much of the pastor's experience may find its faith development limited by that one perspective. There is a great difference between speaking what happens to be on one's mind and giving expression to an idea or experience honed to sharpness by long and serious reflection. The Christian life of the pastor can be the origin of excellent sermon topics as well as a model for the laity, but it is a resource that maintains its power only if used sparingly.

The Sermon

On certain worship occasions, the subject of a sermon will be either broadly or narrowly defined. A community Thanksgiving service, an ecumenical Good Friday observance, or a chapel sermon on a specific subject in a series may present topics not of the preacher's choosing. Many chafe under this type of restriction, but there is valuable discipline in preparing a sermon with little or no choice of subject. It is even more valuable for the pastor to solicit sermon subjects from the congregation and address them. As a rule, when such a solicitation is done, the sermons requested by lay people are on the most elementary and basic themes of the Christian life—the love of God in adversity, forgiveness of others and oneself, guilt, doubt. It is good for us who preach to be driven back to these themes. Given our preferences, we address them too seldom.

The Text

There are many different ways of beginning the sermonic process with a biblical text. One of the most limiting for both preacher and congregation is the repeated turning to a few favorite books or passages. A much richer approach is the following of the lectionary lessons, the lists of Bible readings for each Sunday and holy day recommended for use in worship by many denominations. Even in churches without an official lectionary, the practice is a helpful one for the preacher. Lectionaries draw attention to portions of the Bible that the preacher would not select for preaching if left to his or her own devices. This process of using lectionary readings also permits sermons in series from one book of the Bible. In some churches, sermons for a stretch of Sundays may be taken from a portion or an entire book of the Bible without regard for the lectionary.

The preacher in the midst of study for sermons, classes, and lessons should not neglect devotional reading of the Bible. Again and again, both neophyte and experienced preachers discover new light breaking through from God's book in quiet, personal reading. The discovery of new insights from both familiar and little-known portions of the Bible is one of the most exciting and personally rewarding parts of the preaching ministry.

In practice, the intellectual and creative processes are rarely so stratified that one can pinpoint the precise origin of a single idea. In the great majority of cases, the seed of a sermon will germinate in a mix of soils: an intriguing Bible lesson, a concern expressed in recent pastoral visits, a related article in a pastoral journal, a luncheon conversation with a fellow pastor. Often the creative process is shaped by factors beyond the pastor and parish: World Communion Sunday (occasion), coinciding with a denominational fund drive for world mission (church), and the lectionary Gospel lesson from Luke 24:13–35 (text), with a resulting sermon from verse 35 on the risen Christ being made known to the world in the breaking of bread.

3
Planning a Preaching Schedule

More than one beginning pastor has been intimidated by the seemingly awesome task of coming up with a worthwhile sermon subject every seven days. In sermon preparation, as in other creative endeavors, the secret of discovering fresh and stimulating material is working ahead. The minister who begins each week by asking "What am I going to preach about this Sunday?" will inevitably be latching on to the first idea that comes along (or maybe even secretly sending off to the Instant Sermon Subscription Service: surefire sermons for all churches and occasions, only $89.95 per year, postage paid). For generations, homileticians and veteran preachers have been advising pastors to take time during the summer when parish duties are somewhat lighter to block out sermon themes for the year ahead. This is excellent counsel indeed, and it is a wise preacher who heeds it.

At first glance, planning a preaching program for fifty-two Sundays and numerous special days appears to be a formidable job. But when the year is broken into smaller segments, each with its own theme and focal point, the task is greatly simplified. What follows is a brief for preaching the Christian year, a schedule based on the life of our Lord and on the New Testament church that commemorates the major themes and events in the life of God's people.

For those not accustomed to it, gaining an appreciation of the

Christian year may be a struggle. There are those in the Anabaptist and independent churches who view formalism in worship of any kind as a denial of free church tradition. Some in the Reformed churches regard the observance of specific days and seasons as a confining practice that restrains the power of the Word. There are even those in the more liturgical communions who have always followed the church year but don't know how to make it work for them in the design and performance of pulpit ministry.

The Christian year is by no means complicated or mysterious. In its simplest and most traditional form, it commemorates events and seasons taken directly from the pages of Holy Scripture. Depending on the tradition of his or her church, the preacher may or may not choose to follow the selections for reading from the Bible recommended for each Sunday and other occasions for worship listed in the lectionaries recommended by many denominations. For both the preacher and the congregation, however, faithful observance of the Christian year in the worship life of the church makes the riches of the Bible accessible and provides systematic coverage of the great theological themes.

The Christian Year: A Biblical Corrective for Preaching

It is only a slight exaggeration to say that the preacher must choose what calendar he or she will preach, a calendar based on the life of Christ and the coming of the Holy Spirit or one determined and imposed by the world. The pastor who fails to order the worship life of the congregation according to the great events of the faith is a sitting duck for every secular holiday and observance that comes along. An enduring mystery of the church is the number of congregations that would not dream of celebrating the biblical events of Epiphany, Ascension, and Pentecost in worship and sermon but who annually enter the sanctuary to observe Boy Scout Sunday, Masons' Sunday, Memorial Day, and Mother's Day. Such a program is no more and no less than the proclamation of American civil religion—a triumph of the profane over the sacred.

Commemoration of the cardinal days of the Christian faith lays a solid biblical foundation for the worship and ministry of the local church. All churches celebrate the great festivals of the Nativity and the Resurrection, but the proper spirit of joy and triumph is lacking when the solemn preparatory seasons of Advent and Lent are not observed. Because each day or season has its unique biblical-theological significance, the Christian year is an excellent vehicle for conveying the content of the Bible.

Christian worship has long been enriched by the display of appropriate colors, which are changed according to the season. Thus, as members of the congregation gather in the sanctuary, the visual—in the form of altar cloths, pulpit and lectern hangings, robes and stoles worn by the pastor, and liturgical banners hung on the walls—creates an expectancy that enhances the hearing of the Word in the service of worship. The following brief survey of the Christian year identifies major days and seasons with appropriate biblical and worship themes.

Advent. From the Latin *advenio,* "to come to." This first season of the church calendar begins four Sundays before Christmas and heralds the coming of the Messiah. It is a season of preparation in which the Christian community looks back to the birth of Jesus in Bethlehem and forward to the coming of Christ at the end of history. Proper observance of the season prevents the church from falling into lockstep with the merchandising interests, beginning the observance of Christmas immediately after Thanksgiving. The liturgical color is purple, the color of penitence. Appropriate preaching themes are repentance and preparation for judgment.

Christmas. From the English contraction of "Christ's Mass." Properly celebrated, Christmas is not a single day but a season of twelve days beginning on December 25 and ending on January 6. The theme is the Incarnation, God become flesh. The color is white, symbolizing joy and celebration.

Epiphany. From the Greek *epiphaneia,* "manifestation." Epiphany season runs from January 6, the traditional day of the appearing of the Magi, as recorded in Matthew 2, until Ash Wednesday. The season may therefore include as few as four or as many as eight Sundays. Theologically, the significance is the first manifestation of Christ, the light of the world, to the Gentiles. When Epiphany is celebrated two weeks after Christmas with the reading of Matthew 2:1–12 and the singing of Epiphany hymns, the people can grasp the time interval between the birth of Jesus in a stable and the visitation of the Magi in a house. But when worshipers see manger scenes and Sunday school pageants with the wise men standing at the stable with the shepherds, Epiphany becomes muddled with the Nativity and the teaching of the Bible is distorted. The color on Epiphany Day or the Sunday nearest is white, appropriate because of the star of Bethlehem that pointed the way to Christ. On succeeding Sundays the color is green. The preaching emphasis is properly on the worldwide mission of the church, as God has provided salvation not only for the Jews but for all peoples.

Ash Wednesday. From the biblical application of ashes as a sign of repentance of sin, Ash Wednesday is the first day of Lent.

Lent. The season begins on Ash Wednesday and ends on the Saturday before Easter. The Lenten period includes forty fasting days and six Sundays (Sunday is always a feast day because it is the day of the Resurrection). The forty-day period is drawn from the temptation of Jesus in the wilderness and emphasizes penitence and self-denial in preparation for Easter. (The two greatest festivals in the church year, Christmas and Easter, are both preceded by solemn seasons of preparation.) As in Advent, the color is purple. The preaching stress is on the themes of sacrifice, sorrow for sin, and self-denial. However, there is no reason for worship in this period to be mournful, because Lent always looks forward to Easter and the Resurrection as the hope of the world.

Maundy Thursday. From the Latin *mandatum,* taken from Jesus' words at the Last Supper as recorded in John 15:12: "This is my commandment, that you love one another as I have loved you." As the congregation gathers on "the night when he was betrayed," the people share the Supper on the evening before the crucifixion, just as our Lord instituted it. The sequence and significance of events is largely lost when there is Communion on Good Friday, as is customary in some churches.

Good Friday. The day of crucifixion, the most solemn day in the church's observance. In the Roman Catholic tradition, this is the one day in the year on which Mass may not be celebrated.

Easter. The festival of the Resurrection, the most joyous season of the year. As Jesus remained on earth forty days after being raised, Eastertide is a forty-day season including six Sundays. The color is white, the color of joy and life. Preaching in this season celebrates Christ's victory over death and the power of his resurrection in the church.

Ascension. The celebration of Jesus' ascent into heaven, the validation of his life, ministry, death, and resurrection. Ascension Day falls on Thursday but is most often observed on the following Sunday. The color is white, and the preaching theme is the reign of Christ over creation.

Pentecost. Originally the Feast of Weeks, a Jewish holiday, this date has significance in the Christian tradition as the occasion of the outpouring of the Holy Spirit on the disciples gathered in Jerusalem and the expansion of the church into all the world. The color is red, appropriate to the tongues of fire on the heads of the apostles. Preaching properly centers on the Holy Spirit and the church.

Trinity. Occurring one week after Pentecost, this is the one day in the church year that does not celebrate a biblical event, although it does mark a biblical doctrine. Trinity Sunday was added to the calendar in medieval times to correct an ignorance in the church regarding the triune God. The preaching emphasis is on the Holy Trinity.

In the spring there may be a coinciding of significant sacred and secular days, depending on the date on which Easter falls. Ascension Sunday, Pentecost, and Trinity often conflict with Memorial Day and Mother's Day. Memorial Day, a civic holi-

day to honor those who have died in war, need not be observed in the church. (There is a superb opportunity for
remembering those who have died in the Lord on the Sunday
nearest All Saints' Day, November 1, when the church commemorates the unity of all believers in heaven and on earth
after the teaching of Hebrews 11 and 12. Ironically, the only
seasonal observance in the church at this time is often the
youth group Halloween costume party, which means that the
pagan aspects of the day are retained and the Christian significance is ignored.) Mother's Day is, of course, a creation of the
floral, greeting card, and gift industries. When we read the
sermon titles in the Saturday newspapers the day before, however, we find such chestnuts as "God's Great Gift: Mother-
hood," "The Need for Christian Mothers," or "Godly Moth-
erhood." This is not to deny that there is a need for preaching
on family themes. The pity is that churches will surrender the
great theological truths of the church and the triune God to a
celebration of the commercial.

The season that stretches from late spring until Advent is the
longest in the Christian year and may be designated as Pentecost
or Trinity in various churches. The focus is on the Christian life,
which stems from the great events of the faith celebrated in the
first half of the year. The color is green, the color of nature and
eternal life.

Providing a Balanced Diet for the Flock

In their hearing of the Word of God in worship, the people
need a balanced presentation of the Scriptures. It is therefore
important for the pastor not only to vary the subjects and emphases of sermons but to cover all portions of the Bible as well.
A good standard to follow in laying out a year's preaching
program is the rule of thirds: one third of all sermons should be
preached from the Old Testament, one third from the Gospels
and Acts, and one third from the Epistles and Revelation. In
this way the lay people gain an appreciation for the Bible and
its centrality in the Christian tradition. It is worth remembering
that the kooks and cults that seek to prey on church members

often turn to the Old Testament, proof-texting with obscure passages ripped out of context and then, by means of fantastic hermeneutical leaps, brought to the New Testament and the present. If sermons are never or only rarely preached from the Old Testament, as is the case in some churches, then two thirds of the Bible becomes, by default, a closed book. As a consequence, Christian people are left unequipped to counter the bizarre claims of extremists.

An excellent and simple way to assure variety in a year's preaching schedule is to lay out a series of sermons for each major season of the church year, taking care to balance subjects, emphases, and portions of Scripture. A typical beginning, covering Advent, Epiphany, and Lent, follows. Each sermon is listed according to title, text, and thesis sentence.

Advent and Christmas (Four Sundays and Christmas Eve or Day)

SCRIPTURE: The Gospel of Luke

THEME: Being prepared for Christ to break into our lives

The comings of Jesus in the Gospel narratives make for fascinating reading. People were either unprepared for Jesus when he came or did not know how to respond to him when he arrived. (Matters were made no less complicated by our Lord's habit of ignoring social customs.) Our generation is no different. People in the twentieth century are not prepared for the Second Coming of Christ, nor do they know how to respond to him and his claim on their lives and social order. The preacher today is engaged in the ministry of John the Baptist: preparing the way of the Lord.

Four Advent Sermons on Comings of Jesus in Luke

- "When Jesus Comes to Dinner" (Communion sermon), Luke 5:27–39
  When Jesus sits at his table, all people, regardless of status, are invited to commune with him.

- •"When Jesus Comes to Heal," Luke 8:26–39
  When Jesus comes in power, even the forces of evil must submit to his will.
- •"When Jesus Comes to Preach," Luke 4:16–30
  When Jesus proclaims his Word, it is good news to those ready to hear and accept it; to others it is an offense.
- •"When Jesus Comes to Pray," Luke 19:47–48
  When Jesus comes in judgment to his temple, let us be found faithful in prayer and service.

Christmas Eve or Day

- •"When Jesus Comes to Earth," Luke 2:1–20
  When Jesus comes to his creation, it is the poor and humble who are able to receive him.

Epiphany (Seven Sundays)

SCRIPTURE: 1 Corinthians 1—4 (lectionary lessons for the second year)

THEME: The unity of the church in belief and mission

The coming of the Magi to adore the Christ-child speaks to us not primarily of human aspirations and devotion but of a sovereign God choosing to reveal himself to humankind. The old covenant of the law was given to God's people, the Jews. The new covenant in Christ is given to all the world, Jews and Gentiles alike. The bringing together of people of different races, languages, and traditions created a rich community—but hardly one without problems. The opening chapters of 1 Corinthians can be read as a manual for a church trying to maintain unity in the midst of diversity, a diversity stemming not only from a mix of Jewish and Gentile culture but also from differing life-styles, world views, and role models.

One does not have to read deeply in 1 Corinthians to realize that the problems plaguing the church in its first generation have traveled through the centuries and deposited themselves in our pews. What follows is a series of topics addressing difficulties in the church that crop up again and again.

- •"Looking the Gift Horse in the Mouth," 1 Corinthians 1:1–9
  God, from his abundance, has given the church every gift it needs to perform its mission.
- •"Preventive Medicine," 1 Corinthians 1:10–17
  The greatest threat to church unity is not theological differences but identification with human personalities.
- •"Back to Reality," 1 Corinthians 1:18–25
  At Christmas we read the Gospels, which begin with birth narratives, but Paul begins his epistle with the cross.
- •"The Foundation of Faith," 1 Corinthians 2:1–5
  The church is a divine-human institution that is rooted in God's power rather than in human wisdom.
- •"What's a Bright Person Like You Doing in a Place Like This?" 1 Corinthians 2:6–13
  Popular thinking produces the spirit of this world; mature wisdom creates in us the mind of Christ.
- •"Reviewing the Plans," 1 Corinthians 3:10–23
  God has provided for us the foundation and plans for our lives, but the building is our responsibility.
- •"The Perfect Judge," 1 Corinthians 4:1–5
  It is not our responsibility to judge others, or even ourselves, but to submit to the perfect judgment of God.

Lent and Easter (Seven Sundays)

SCRIPTURE: Jonah and Ezekiel

THEME: Redemption, personal and corporate

The Lenten season, based traditionally on the wilderness temptation of Jesus, is a time for preaching on the difficult issues of the Christian life. We need to remember, however, that Lent is not preparation for Good Friday but preparation for Easter. Thus our message in this season is ultimately not one of crucifixion but of resurrection. Our Lord has not called us to share his cross without also promising that we shall be raised with him.

The sermons from Jonah are a character study of the prophet, each dealing with a crisis of personal experience from the four chapters of the prophecy. The remaining two sermons for Lent and the Easter sermon are taken from Ezekiel and address the corporate experience of Judah and the people of the new covenant, the church.

- "The Crisis of Self-Awareness: Who Am I?" Jonah 1
  Even when we are beset by questions of identity, purpose, and self-worth, God's claim is upon our lives.
- "The Crisis of Self-Despair: Is There No Hope?" Jonah 2
  If we open ourselves to God, he is able to free us from the prisons of our guilt.
- "The Crisis of Self-Will: What Has God Done?" Jonah 3
  Repentance is not only an act for nonbelievers but a continuous spirit that allows us to experience God's mercy.
- "The Crisis of Self-Pity: Why Me?" Jonah 4
  The Lord may chasten us in times of despair so that we can change our focus from ourselves to his purpose for us.
- "Small Beginnings," Ezekiel 17:22
  God has promised deliverance to his people not in a great, dramatic act but in the planting of a young twig.
- "When Death Ends in Life," Ezekiel 37:1–14 (Palm/Passion Sunday)
  At the very worst of times, when there is absolutely no hope, God calls us to proclaim the message of life.
- "New Heart, New Spirit, New Life!" Ezekiel 36:16–28 (Easter)
  God acts on our behalf, not for our sakes but to show his majesty and power.

This blocking out of a preaching schedule could continue with Eastertide sermons from 1 John on overcoming the world with the love given at the Resurrection, a Pentecost series on the power of the Holy Spirit in the church from Acts, and a summer sequence on favorite psalms. The sermon themes presented for

Advent, Epiphany, and Lent should be sufficient to show the potential benefits of a well-planned program that draws from different portions of the Bible and addresses a variety of subjects.

Advantages of Preaching in Series

Preparation. The pastor can save much study time. In the sermons from 1 Corinthians and Jonah for Epiphany and Lent, for example, the exegetical work for several sermons can be done in a few days. Then, as the series unfolds week by week, the pastor can develop each sermon from that research without returning to the reference books.

Worship. When the pastor works well in advance, those with worship responsibilities can also plan ahead. This is a great help to the people who select hymns, anthems, and instrumental works appropriate to the worship theme established by the sermon.

Education. With adequate planning, the educational ministry and preaching program of the church can strengthen each other. Classes and discussion groups can work on texts and themes both before and after the sermon is preached in worship.

Spiritual Development. The listening congregation gains a more complete knowledge of biblical doctrines and themes when sermons have continuity. As a result, the laity is better equipped to think theologically and to read the Bible more intelligently.

Some Cautions About Preaching in Series

Integrity. Even in a series, each sermon needs to have its own sense of purpose. Unlike a television miniseries that leaves the audience hanging every week and resolves everything in the final episode, each sermon needs its own climax and resolution.

Scope. For the most part, a series is in the mind of the preacher. Lay people may not be aware of the precise fit of each sermonic jewel in the golden setting of the series—and they do not need to be. It is far more important that they appreciate the big picture and gain an overview of the biblical message.

Brevity. A sermon series should be brief if it is to retain interest. The preacher who devotes several months to preaching through Isaiah, Matthew, or Romans usually ends up not only with a bored congregation but with a bored preacher. A better way to cover an entire book is in several short series over a period of a few years.

Flexibility. The preacher should never feel bound by her or his own schedule. Events or issues that need to be addressed from the pulpit arise with little or no notice, requiring the pastor to exercise judgment on departing from announced plans.

Sharpening the Subject

Most sermons are conceived with only a general sense of subject. A general statement is adequate for listing on a preaching schedule, but as the date of each sermon approaches, the pastor begins preparation with a sharpening of the preliminary subject. In the great majority of cases, this work can be completed in thirty minutes using only an English Bible.

The importance of this task should not be minimized, for the failure to refine and sharpen the subject of the sermon is probably the greatest single shortcoming in the work of beginning preachers. However, simple safeguards can be built into the homiletical process that will help the pastor make the sermon definite in subject and pointed in application. For purposes of example, the following paragraphs apply three such principles or safeguards to the text and preliminary subject chosen for the Fifth Sunday after Epiphany: 1 Corinthians 2:6–13.

First, Examine the Setting of the Text

This examination is a cursory overview of the context of the sermon lesson, as opposed to the more thorough consideration of contextual issues done later in the exegetical work. In order to determine the teaching of the text for the sermon, the preacher establishes the setting of the biblical lesson: To whom was this written? By whom? For what reason? What was happening in the lives of the writer and the readers at the time? How does this lesson relate to those immediately preceding and following? Many additional questions could be added, but these are sufficient to sharpen the subject.

The general teaching of 1 Corinthians 2:6–13 is that wisdom is a gift from God given by his Spirit. Paul addressed this teaching to a congregation he knew well. Corinth was a seaport, a wealthy, hard-living, cosmopolitan center of commerce. Because Corinth was a crossroads of the ancient world, there was no shortage of itinerant religious leaders, educators, philosophers, and teachers clamoring for a hearing. The Hellenistic culture glorified a concept of wisdom based on education and intellectual attainment, and this thinking had currency in the Corinthian church. In chapter 1, Paul writes that the wisdom of the world is confounded by the cross; in chapter 3, he urges the new believers in Corinth to absorb the simple lessons of the faith, that they might gain strength to overcome problems of jealousy and strife.

Paul's teaching, we see, was intended to correct an attitude that defined wisdom in intellectual rather than spiritual terms. The person who is not spiritual is never able to understand those who have been given wisdom according to God's Spirit. As we look toward the sermon, this text gives us an excellent opportunity to compare and contrast wisdom as conceived and understood by the society, and wisdom as received and experienced by the Christian.

Second, Limit the Scope of the Theme

As the sermon model in chapter 1 shows (Figure 1), the preacher does not address the entire human situation with a single homiletical blast. The preacher targets one aspect of human experience—an attitude, emotion, value, goal, feeling, belief—and examines it in the light of an appropriate portion of Scripture. When that target aspect has been selected, it will invariably have to be reduced in order to be manageable.

The general subject of our sermon is wisdom as a gift of the Spirit bestowed by God. In both its biblical and contemporary usage, "wisdom" is a broad term. In our generation, wisdom is often confused with education, occupation, notoriety, or social standing; the sermon will need to clear away these stereotypes. (The ancient Hebrews would not have been so naive as to assume that the conferring of a Ph.D. makes a person wise!) This popular assumption often leaves church people with feelings of intellectual inferiority, particularly in parishes in urban centers and university communities. The brightest and most educated people are the most wise, goes the premise, but many if not most of these "wise" people are not to be found in the church. Therefore, comes the conclusion, since those who are "wise" are not found in the church, those who are found in church must be less wise.

The language of the text marks a distinct contrast: "wisdom of this age," "rulers of this age," "spirit of the world," "human wisdom," and "the unspiritual man," as against "among the mature," "a secret and hidden wisdom," "the Spirit which is from God," "those who possess the Spirit." The structure and wording of the text and a breakdown of the subject are parallel tracks leading to a sermon contrasting worldly and spiritual wisdom.

Third, Reflect on the Experience of the Congregation

At this point the pastor should ask, "Who needs to hear this sermon?" It is helpful to take a pad of paper and jot down initials of parishioners for whom the sermon will have particular relevance: a university student who is struggling with doubt because his psychology professors can explain all religious experience in emotional terms; a middle-aged woman who is treated with condescension by her professional family because she alone "needs the church"; a recently widowed man, embittered in his grief, who only last week said, "I sure don't understand God and what he does. Most people I know don't bother with God at all;

maybe they know more than I do." As the preparation proceeds, the pastor can pray for these people—specifically, that they will benefit from the sermon. And because we are members of the congregation too (set apart for the task of ministry), it is appropriate that we include ourselves in the listing of those who need to hear. We must never lose the sense of being under the discipline of the Word or fail to pray that we will be challenged and strengthened by the preaching of it.

This brief interaction with text, topic, and congregation can be the most important half hour in the preparation of the sermon. If the preacher proceeds too soon to exegetical work and beyond without a clear, sharp, and limited subject, much time will be wasted on ideas and data that are not appropriate to the central theme of the sermon.

As for our example, the subject when sharpened was expressed as listed earlier in the sermons for the Epiphany season: Popular thinking produces the spirit of this world; mature wisdom creates in us the mind of Christ. The sermon, entitled "What's a Bright Person Like You Doing in a Place Like This?", was developed around two major points, popular thinking and mature wisdom. But we're getting ahead of ourselves. Organizing sermon materials into a cogent and cohesive whole is the subject of the next chapter.

4
Organizing the Discourse

For more than half a century, writers on the homiletical craft have made the subject of sermon structure a good deal more complicated than it need be. Much of our thinking and practice carries over from the Victorian period, when sermons were characterized by an ornate style that is, by today's standards, artificial. When sermons routinely lasted forty-five minutes or more, however, there was a need for detailed organizational structure that would carry the weight of the preacher's argument and maintain the interest of the congregation.

We live in a day of shortened attention spans. While we may decry a state of affairs in which people are unwilling or unable to listen to oral presentations for longer than thirty minutes or so, the fact remains that we live and preach not in an ideal world but in a real one. People's listening habits are conditioned not so much by the church as by radio and television. A half-hour situation comedy, a one-hour drama, a two-hour movie, or a three-hour football game is interrupted every ten or fifteen minutes for commercials. People come to expect such breaks and are conditioned by them to absorb information in small doses.

In the last century, the content of a one-hour sermon would typically have been apportioned as follows: ten minutes for an introduction, with biblical and classical allusions; fifteen minutes for a description of the problem or issue; twenty minutes of exposition of the biblical text; and fifteen minutes of application.

A contemporary sermon is likely to be twenty minutes or even less in length. The preacher of today does not enjoy the luxury of the leisurely introduction complete with literary and scriptural images, the detailed analysis of the problem, the thorough working with the text, and the wide-ranging application. We must proclaim the Word to the most overstimulated generation in history, and in only half or even a third of the time commanded by our ancestors in the pulpit. As a result, our structures must be leaner and simpler than those of a century ago.

Purposes of Sermon Arrangement

The primary function of sermon organization is to allow the essential biblical message to be proclaimed with clarity and power. Sound sermon structure never calls attention to itself but focuses the message on human need, biblical exposition, and Christian action. A well-structured sermon assists the listeners by providing a sense of unity, coherence, and emphasis.

Unity. All material in the sermon should relate to the central purpose. When the sermon is well constructed, both the preacher in preparation and the congregation in listening can perceive the interrelation of biblical exposition, illustrations, quotations, and application to the theme.

Coherence. If it is to be understood, a sermon needs to be a coherent and comprehensible whole. Ideas should build on each other in orderly and logical fashion.

Emphasis. The major components of the sermon (introduction, body, conclusion) should be constructed so that the significance of each part stands out and has its own identity. It is especially important not only that there be a sense of movement but also that the argument build to a strong and convincing conclusion.

Advantages of Sound Arrangement

The pastor who takes care in assembling the sermon will reap immediate and lasting benefits in the study, the pulpit, and the sanctuary.

Preparation in the Study. The preacher who is able to write a clear subject sentence and move quickly to at least a rough outline will save much time in gathering, organizing, and writing. One of the most important tasks of the preacher is editing. In the formative stages of every sermon there is material that needs to be cut and perhaps saved for another Sunday. If early in the preparation the preacher can work up a preliminary structure with main headings to go with the subject, then appropriate material can be retained and inappropriate data eliminated.

Memory in the Pulpit. In the moment of delivery, a well-organized sermon is far easier to remember and preach than a poorly structured one. Even without an outline or typescript, the preacher who has carefully crafted the sermon will usually be able to return to the flow when concentration is broken or memory fails. (All veteran pastors have favorite tales of trying to retrieve the message after a memory lapse.) And because it is all but impossible to remember a disorganized sermon, it is an excellent check on your exercise to preach an occasional sermon without notes or manuscript.

Credibility in the Pew. Repeated studies in the communication field report that the single most important factor in persuasion is the regard in which the audience holds the speaker. In the minds of the listeners, the quality of the sermon and the action it advocates are inextricably bound to the personal credibility of the preacher. A disorganized and incomprehensible sermon reflects badly on the pastor both as a preacher and as a person. A clearly ordered and comprehensible message reflects well on the preacher and is far more likely to have its desired effect.

Approaches to Arrangement

Even before we write an outline, it is necessary to determine the overall thought pattern of the sermon. How and when does the preacher want the congregation to perceive the thesis? That is, will the sermon be *deductive,* addressing its subject directly at the outset and then offering specific support of the thesis? Or should the sermon progress according to an *inductive* pattern, building on specific arguments to a general statement of the thesis at the conclusion? One approach is not to be preferred over the other, but the preacher should exercise some care in matching the type of arrangement to the subject matter of the sermon.

The difference between the two approaches can be simply shown.

Deductive pattern
  General thesis
    There is racism in our community
  Specific support
    There are no local minority-owned businesses
    Real-estate people turn away minority property seekers
    Unemployment is 12 percent higher among minorities than
      Caucasians
    Our churches have only a handful of minority members
Inductive pattern
  Specific support
    There are no local minority-owned businesses
    Real-estate people turn away minority property seekers
    Unemployment is 12 percent higher among minorities than
      Caucasians
    Our churches have only a handful of minority members
  General thesis
    There is racism in our community

Deductive Arrangement

The great majority of communications we see and hear are deductive in pattern. That is, the general thesis is presented and the specific supporting arguments follow. Particularly in education, government, business, and industry, where time is money and clarity is of the essence, the deductive method is all-pervasive. In the Bible, Paul's sermon on Mars Hill (Acts 17:22–31) displays a deductive process of argumentation. After the obligatory visiting speaker's introduction about the local landscape, in which he extends the Athenians a backhanded compliment for their religious fervor, Paul states the thesis of his sermon: "What therefore you worship as unknown, this I proclaim to you." The apostle then presents the brief for the God who is Lord of heaven and earth. This God, rather than being made with human hands, has in fact created humanity: the Scriptures and Greek poets are quoted in support; the commandment of God to repent to avoid judgment and gain resurrection is the motivational conclusion.

The chief advantage of deduction is its clarity. When hearers know the point of the sermon from the outset, they can evaluate and apply the succeeding support material to the already-presented thesis. The bane of perfect clarity is utter predictability, and a sermon that is totally predictable seldom sparkles. "My subject today is————and I am going to develop it as follows" may be an appropriate beginning for an academic lecture, but in a sermon a first sentence like that will surely produce yawns all through the sanctuary.

Inductive Arrangement

The opposite of the deductive approach is a pattern of reasoning that moves from specific arguments to a general conclusion or thesis statement. The Hebrew mind, unsullied by hard-sell thirty-second commercials, tedious journal articles, and straight-to-the-point office memos, rather enjoyed the more leisurely inductive approach. The classic biblical examples of inductive homilies are the parables of Jesus. When preaching on status and the equality of all persons in the Kingdom of God, Jesus related the parable of the householder (Matt. 20:1–16). "For the kingdom of heaven is like . . ." begins the sermon: a householder is hiring laborers who go into the vineyard at various times of the day; some work long hours in the heat; others work only in the cool of the evening; all are paid equally; those who toiled longest complain; the householder reminds them of their contract. And the general conclusion? In the Kingdom, "the last will be first, and the first last."

A key strength of the inductive approach is that it exploits the greatest of human weaknesses: curiosity. (Who can forget that David was so burning with curiosity to learn the identity of the sheep-stealing rich man that he stepped right into Nathan's meticulously prepared inductive trap? David himself was the rich man, Bathsheba the ewe lamb, and Uriah the poor man; 2 Sam. 12:1–15.) We want to learn the point of the story, lesson, sermon, or whatever. The flip side of curiosity, however, is impatience: we will stay with a message without knowing the point for only so long. Biblical people lived before movable type made its imprint not only on paper but also on our thought processes. An oral society communicates by the story, song, epic, poem, acrostic, or parable. Since the invention of movable type by Gutenberg, our literate society expects its communications, both written and oral, to be straightforward and linear, with the meaning up front. The pastor who utilizes a fresh approach and delivers a well-constructed inductive sermon can gain a hearing by breaking the communications stereotype.

Inductive-Deductive Arrangement

Deduction and induction are not mutually exclusive entities; in fact, they are commonly used in combination in the same sermon. In a problem–solution type of development, for example, the first half may proceed inductively, building item on specific item to a statement of general principle at the midpoint. The second half then elaborates on the theme and develops the solution with specific material.

The sermon from Romans 8:18–25 later in this chapter is structured in just this way. The introduction raises the question of why there is evil in the world. The first major point proceeds inductively to answer the question. The second major point begins with the affirmation of hope in our redemption in Christ and supports that affirmation to the conclusion.

Components of Sermon Structure

The homiletical literature in our generation gives evidence of an appropriate and healthy reaction to the sermon forms that were handed down to us. Those who write on preaching today are more likely to advocate inductive, narrative, and story approaches to the sermon, as opposed to the overworked deductive model of an earlier time when the preacher would state a premise and then march through a series of propositions to an inevitable and often foregone conclusion. But variety remains the spice of life. There is room in the sanctuary for a great many sermonic forms, and the preacher is well advised to make use of them.

No matter what type of arrangement is employed, however, and no matter how far the preacher wants to go to avoid traditional structures, it is difficult if not impossible to escape the need in a sermon for three essential structural components: the *introduction,* the *body,* and the *conclusion.* There is no need to fall into the all-too-common didactic mentality that the introduction states the thesis of the sermon, the body develops and explains the thesis, and the conclusion restates it. (This is the old "First I tell 'em what I'm gonna tell 'em; then I tell 'em; then I tell 'em what I told 'em" approach.) This model institutionalizes repetition and is a sure ticket to boredom.

The three components of the sermon serve three quite different functions. The introduction presents the issue being addressed; the body develops that issue and provides an answer; the conclusion motivates people to action.

A model revealing both the independence and interdependence of the three components was developed by Professor Henry Babcock Adams for his students at San Francisco Theological Seminary. With a goal of achieving maximum clarity, the Adams formula reduces the sermon to three sentences: a *question,* an *assertion,* and an *invitation,* which correspond to the three essential components, the introduction, the body, and the conclusion.

Question. Every sermon addresses an issue or problem which can be stated in the interrogative and raised in the introduction.

Our example from Romans 8:18–25 begins with the question "If God is good, why is there evil in the world?" The question is stated in simple, direct language that requires an answer.

Assertion. The question is answered with a thesis, premise, or truth developed in the body of the sermon. This answer, drawn from the teaching of the biblical text, addresses the issues posed by the question. The assertion for the Romans 8 sermon is "God has chosen to subject his creation to futility, but he will also redeem it in hope."

Invitation. After the question has been raised and answered, the congregation is called to response by the conclusion. Herein lies the difference between a lecture and a sermon. The lecturer is finished after posing a question and providing an answer. The preacher must go one step further and motivate the congregation to action. Because the stress is on action, the invitation will be hortatory in nature and usually expressed in the imperative or subjunctive mood. To complete our example, the invitation states, "Let us wait patiently for God's hope."

The entire three-sentence formula, listed under the text, appears as follows:

TEXT: Romans 8:18–25

QUESTION (introduction): If God is good, why is there evil in the world?

ASSERTION (body): God has chosen to subject his creation to futility, but he will finally redeem it in hope.

INVITATION (conclusion): Let us wait patiently for God's hope.

The formula not only states the sermon thesis in capsule form, it also reveals the thematic flow. This can be of great help to the preacher, who, with this valuable tool, can check the progression from beginning to end: Is the *question* clear? Does the *assertion* address the issue raised by the question? Does the *invitation* urge action appropriate to the question and assertion?

Models of Sermon Structure

We learn to talk in infancy. Instruction in public address, for those few who receive it, comes much later. Although we think and converse in essentially linear patterns, it is an unusual person indeed who outlines personal thoughts and conversations. If a verbatim record were kept of our conversations for one day, we would find them filled with interruptions, interjections, digressions, sudden subject changes, repetitions, and the like. It is the nature of face-to-face interaction that we are able to question, clarify, and respond so that these nonfluencies usually present no significant barrier to clear communication. Speaking to an audience is an entirely different matter, however, and those nonfluencies so common in personal conversation are extremely disconcerting in public address.

Inasmuch as most students have been talking for twenty years or more before their first instruction in public speaking (or homiletics), learning to structure ideas before expressing them can be difficult, and lessons in how to write outlines can be the dullest of all. It is not the intent of this chapter to wade through the steps of preparing a sermon outline. Rather, five sample sermons follow, in outline form, with commentary accompanying each. In each sermon, the flow of the outline follows the line of action or reasoning in the text. It is hoped that the student of preaching, by reading the text and seeing an overview of the structure of the message, will grasp the interrelation of biblical text and sermon.

These outlines should *not* be read with the sense that there are five and only five types of sermon arrangements. The only limit to sermon approaches is that imposed by human imagination. Nor is it claimed that these efforts represent the only, best, or preferred way to preach from each text.

The reader will have to contend with the usual limitation of reading outlines. The placement of illustrations and quotations is indicated, but limited space prevents recording them in their entirety. The same is true, in most cases, of the introductions and conclusions.

The outlines as they appear should be sufficiently complete

to give the reader a sense not only of the theme and flow of the sermon but also of the practice of drawing the arrangement of the sermon from the structure of the biblical text. Note that the five sermons here presented are traditional in format. Each has a distinct introduction, body, and conclusion as well as identifiable major points. There are, of course, newer, more innovative sermonic forms that largely dispense with this type of structure, and preachers should be encouraged to experiment with such forms. A parallel may be drawn between learning to preach and learning to paint. The beginning artist, before tackling expressionism and abstractionism, learns traditional methods. Seemingly innumerable hours are spent sketching, drawing, shading, and even copying the classics, to achieve mastery of technique. Only when the student has conquered the basics may he or she go on to more individualistic style. The same is true of preachers. Those who are successful in developing and using creative homiletical forms are invariably those who first mastered the traditional patterns of sermon construction.

"The Crisis of Self-Will: What Has God Done?"

TEXT:	Jonah 3
OCCASION:	Third Sunday in Lent
DEVELOPMENT:	Inductive
QUESTION:	Why does God so often act in ways that surprise and frustrate us?
ASSERTION:	God alone is sovereign, and his will is not bound by ours.
INVITATION:	Let us be subject to God's will and do his work.
INTRODUCTION:	Re-creation of Jonah making travel arrangements to Nineveh after earlier journey to Tarshish.

TRANSITION: The word of the Lord came to Jonah
the second time because he missed it
the first time. Had it been necessary,
the word of the Lord would have come
to Jonah a third, a fourth, or even a
fifth time—Jonah had been chosen by
God, and he could not escape his calling. There unfolds, then, a drama in
three acts, each act featuring a different hero who takes center stage, repents of the past, and turns to a new
course of action.

I. THE PROPHET REPENTS (Act I)
  A. Jonah's repentance
    1. Repentance: stereotypes
      ILLUSTRATION: Dendrites, Simeon Stylites, Luther,
      revivalists
    2. Repentance: biblical teaching
  B. Jonah's obedience
II. THE KING REPENTS (Act II)
  A. The king's repentance
    1. Sackcloth and ashes
      a. Biblical use
        QUOTE: Job to Zophar: "Your maxims are proverbs
        of ashes"
      b. Present use
        QUOTE: JFK: "The fruits of victory in nuclear war
        would turn to ashes in our mouths"
  B. The king's example to the people
III. THE LORD REPENTS (Act III)
  A. The Lord's repentance
    1. Visible outward signs
    2. Invisible inward spirit
  B. The Lord's restraint

CONCLUSION: God is merciful and stands ready to
forgive those who repent and call on
him. Our responsibility is clear: God
calls us to repent of our indifference

and even hostility to other people, that
they may hear the gospel and respond
to his love.

Arrangement. The chronological outline proceeds according
to the unfolding of events in the text. This ordering refers not
to a sequence of topics in non-narrative portions of the Bible
(such as the Epistles) but to actual happenings in time. It is
presupposed, therefore, that the text contains a story line.

Exegetical Note. In this second call of Jonah, no mention is
made of his earlier disobedience. As the narrative unfolds, three
highly improbable characters repent: Jonah the prophet repents
of his willfulness, the king of Nineveh repents of his sin (and
subsequently the people do so as well), and the Lord repents of
his promised destruction of the city. The point of the chapter
is that repentance that results in changed conduct will see the
lifting of God's sentence of judgment. Jonah was left frustrated
and angry by the Lord's change of heart because his prophecy
didn't come to pass, thus jeopardizing his credibility as a
prophet.

Design. As this is one of the most dramatic chapters in the
Bible, the imagery of the theater is used to highlight the three
penitents and their acts of repentance. The action builds as each
character is a less likely candidate for repentance than the one
before.

Thesis. Our people have a distorted view of repentance, based
on the stereotypical emotional appeals by revivalists to walk the
sawdust trail. The illustrations in I.A, beginning with the Den-
drites, an early Christian sect whose members lived in trees as
a form of self-denial, are a survey of inadequate conceptions of
repentance in the history of the church. After clearing away a
simplistic and erroneous definition of repentance as a once-only
negative act, the sermon presents the biblical teaching of repentance as a lifelong attitude of turning toward God. As we live in
a penitent and contrite spirit, an emphasis appropriate to the
Lenten season, we experience God's mercy and forgiveness
again and again.

"Who Are We?"

TEXT:	1 Peter 2:1–10
OCCASION:	Fifth Sunday after Easter
DEVELOPMENT:	Deductive
QUESTION:	What is our purpose in gathering together as a small congregation?
ASSERTION:	We are God's people, chosen by him to be built into his church.
INVITATION:	Let us be God's people in the world.
INTRODUCTION:	Research into family origins has become a big business. Americans by the thousands are tracing their ancestry to find out who they are and where they have come from. For a religious, ethnic, or racial minority group, identity is essential to survival. The apostle Peter wrote to an oppressed group of small churches in Asia Minor. Those early Christians were feeling the lash of persecution, and Peter knew they must have a sense of spiritual identity if they were to survive and prosper.
TRANSITION:	If Peter had submitted his epistle as an essay in a high school English course, he would have received an F, for he addressed his readers with a strange mixed metaphor of babies and stones.

I. BABIES
    A. Need for youthful faith in Asia Minor
        1. Small churches
        2. Scattered congregations
        3. Hostile forces
    B. Need for youthful faith in our situation
        1. Small churches

    2. Scattered congregations
    3. Hostile forces
    QUOTE: Matthew 18:3
II. STONES
  A. Quality
    1. Christ as stone
      a. Cornerstone
      b. Stumbling stone
    2. Living stones for the church
      ILLUSTRATION: New England stone walls built by Confederate POWs
  B. Quantity
    1. Many stones are needed to build the structure on the cornerstone
      ILLUSTRATION: Advice of retired stonemason on stone construction
    2. God has chosen us as living stones to be built on his Son to complete his chcomplete his church

CONCLUSION: The purpose of Peter's mixed metaphor is to affirm the value of people. "Once you were no people," he writes. "Now you are God's people." Armed with a youthful faith and the confidence of being chosen by God for his church, let us be his people in the world.

Arrangement. Topical organization features separate headings according to topics or categories in the text. In a lesson such as this one, in which there is no story or action and the content is potentially abstract, specific topics within the text can provide a structural vehicle. No temporal or sequential order is implied in this arrangement, although topics are usually considered as they appear in the text.

Exegetical Note. 1 Peter is a general epistle addressed to several struggling churches in Asia Minor during a time of sporadic rather than systematic persecution. The letter is meant to encourage the readers in their newly embraced faith and instill in them a sense of identity as Christians. The babies-milk imagery urges ardor and growth in the faith. The living stones motif not only is tied to Christ as the cornerstone but also provides a contrast of the believers as living stones over against the dead stones of pagan temples.

Design. The introduction exploits the current interest in genealogies and origins and the pride created in people, families, and groups who know their roots. Peter's strange mix of metaphors provides the major headings. The exhortations of the text for a youthful, resilient faith, and living stones to be built into a strong church, are as appropriate today as when they were written.

Thesis. We live in a society that glorifies bigness for its own sake. Unfortunately, this mentality has found its way into the church. Many small congregations are made to feel inferior because they are not super-churches and never will be. The Bible tells us that a great church is characterized by a vibrant and growing faith in Christ, not necessarily a church big in numbers. This sermon was planned as a shot in the arm for a New England congregation of approximately one hundred people in the Easter season.

"Doubtful Reason and Reasonable Doubt"

TEXT:	John 21:15–17; 20:24–29
OCCASION:	University chapel service
DEVELOPMENT:	Inductive/deductive
QUESTION:	Why is it that even when our faith is strongest, we still experience doubt?
ASSERTION:	We are not saved by our perfect faith, and doubt will always be a part of our experience.
INVITATION:	Let us follow the risen Christ, not in the confidence of our own faith but in the certainty of God's faithfulness.

INTRODUCTION: Narrative on John 21

TRANSITION: Peter's confidence

QUOTE: Francis Bacon on certainty

I. DOUBTFUL REASON
  A. The nature of "certain" faith
     ILLUSTRATION: Pop poster: "Repent"
  B. The nature of Peter's faith
     1. Peter's loyalty
     2. Peter's failure
II. REASONABLE DOUBT
  A. The nature of Thomas's faith
     1. Thomas's loyalty
     2. Thomas's skepticism
  B. The nature of contemporary faith
     1. The confidence of science
        ILLUSTRATION: Russian university students doubting materialism and exploring Christianity. Doubt in the mind trained to examine, question, and challenge is inevitable. Because it is inevitable, it is reasonable doubt, but we may take comfort, for it is a doubt that we share with the apostles themselves.
     2. The sufficiency of the Resurrection
        a. The desire for stability
        b. The imperative for change

TRANSITION: Can we see our own experience in the post-Easter events?

CONCLUSION: So let us follow the risen Christ, not in the self-confident spirit of doubtful reason but in the conscious awareness of reasonable doubt, secure in the knowledge that God is faithful and his love is sufficient to save us all.

Arrangement. Cause-and-effect relationships (and effect-to-cause as well) are usually presented in two-part structures. When the movement is from cause to effect, the presentation will be chronological; in effect-to-cause organization the sermon will work back in time. This sermon features a pair of cause-and-effect relationships: (I) doubtful reason causes a crisis of faith; (II) reasonable doubt gives rise to a healthy faith.

Exegetical Note. This pair of post-Easter lessons provides a fascinating contrast in the faith experience of two disciples, Peter and Thomas. Only a few days before this breakfast on the beach, Simon Peter, stung by Jesus' prophecy of denial, had confidently sworn his loyalty, only to fall before the questions of a maid outside the meeting of the Sanhedrin. Now Jesus had pursued Peter to the lake and extracted from him three affirmations of love corresponding to his three denials. Thomas, meanwhile, has been taking a bad rap as a doubter for some nineteen centuries. Knowing that those closest to Jesus had consistently misunderstood his mission and purposes, Thomas wanted evidence before committing himself to his colleagues' claim of a resurrection.

Design. In addition to the double cause-and-effect arrangement within the two major headings, the sermon moves from the incorrect (doubtful reason) to the correct (reasonable doubt). Preaching from more than one text can be tricky, but the contrasts presented in these post-Resurrection stories make the effort worthwhile.

Thesis. The sermon was preached in a university chapel. Student faith is inevitably accompanied by doubt, and many a crisis of belief has been compounded by well-intentioned Christians who "assure" struggling sisters and brothers that if their faith were only stronger, they would have no doubts. The fact that those closest to Jesus, who saw him after his triumph over death, still experienced doubt should be a source of comfort to us. We remain incapable of perfection, even in faith.

"What's the Use?"

TEXT:	Romans 8:18–25
OCCASION:	Fifth Sunday of Easter

DEVELOPMENT: Inductive/deductive

QUESTION: If God is good, why is there evil in the
                      world?

ASSERTION: God has chosen to subject his creation
                      to futility, but he will finally redeem it
                      in hope.

INVITATION: Let us wait patiently for God's hope.

INTRODUCTION: In recent months we have learned
                      more than we ever wanted to know
                      about nuclear destruction. Scientists,
                      politicians, doctors, television pro-
                      grams, and church bodies are sound-
                      ing dire warnings about the threat of
                      nuclear war. A question often asked is,
                      "Where is God when humankind
                      builds weapons of mass annihilation?"

QUOTE: David Hume: God is either not all-
                      powerful or not all-good.

I. SUBJECTION TO FUTILITY
   A. How?
      1. Creation perfect (Gen. 1:31)
      2. First-century Rome: Jews persecuted
      3. Threats of annihilation in every age
   B. Why?
      1. Some blame God
         ILLUSTRATION: Enzo Ferrari on God as evil force
      2. Paul blames human sin
         QUOTE: Psychologist on devil's work being done 24
         hours a day
II. SUBJECTION TO HOPE
   A. God reaches out to humanity with unseen hope
      1. To Adam, Abraham, Moses, David, and Isaiah in the
         Old Covenant
      2. To us in Christ
         a. False expectations of Roman Christians
         b. False expectations of contemporary Christians

ILLUSTRATION: American civil religion
B. We reach out to God with unseen faith

CONCLUSION: Quote from JFK inaugural: "Let us
                       begin. . . ." We are to wait and work
                       with patience.

Arrangement. The problem solution or need-plan approach is
quite similar in construction to the causal model of organization. There are usually two major sections: an analysis or description of a problem, followed by a solution to that problem.
A variation of this theme is the expansion of the problem step
to two or more extreme points of view and the presentation of
a biblical alternative.

Exegetical Note. The first Christians walked a tenuous line in
their relations with the Roman Empire. As long as they were
perceived as a branch of Judaism, the followers of Christ did not
have to bow to the emperor's image and were relatively secure.
When the two beliefs were seen as distinct religious entities,
however, the infant church had much to fear. As pressures on
the congregation in Rome increased, and severe persecution
drew nearer, Paul wrote to the church in its concern and despair.

Design. The simple problem-solution structure is taken from
verse 20, with its language of a double subjection of creation: to
futility and to hope. The introduction establishes our mood of
despair with the nuclear sword of Damocles hanging over the
world. This mood continues in the first major section of the
body with how and why creation was subjected to futility. At
the midpoint of the sermon, verse 20 is restated and the subjection of creation in hope is introduced.

Thesis. Beginning with the first Christians in Rome, every
generation of believers has been well aware of the sense of
futility in the created order. Everyone has faced its equivalent
of nuclear holocaust: invading barbarians, the Black Death,
repressive government. With scant evidence of a better world,
the apostle urged the Romans to a life of hope in doing God's

work. Even when futility surrounds us and hope seems far from us, we are encouraged in like manner.

"The Gift Shop"

TEXT:	1 Corinthians 12:1–13, 27–31
OCCASION:	Seminary chapel service
DEVELOPMENT:	Inductive
QUESTION:	Why does the exercise of some gifts of the Spirit cause disruption in the body of Christ?
ASSERTION:	The gifts of the Spirit are for the strengthening of the body.
INVITATION:	Let us use our gifts to strengthen the body of Christ.
INTRODUCTION:	Two years ago as commencement approached, one of my senior advisees began the process of being interviewed by pulpit committees. He came to me after his initial interview rather shaken by the experience, because the first question put to him was, "Do you speak in tongues?" The question was asked in such a way that he knew the interview would be over if he gave the wrong answer. His is an experience that has been shared by many of our graduates, as the entire question of speaking in tongues is a source of much tension in the church.

I. TONGUES: A GIFT OF THE SPIRIT
  A. Survey of erroneous attitudes
    1. Seminary president: 95 percent psychological, 5 percent demonic

2. Theologian: for the New Testament age only
3. Seminary student: wishes all would speak in tongues
4. Talk-show host: no Christian experience without tongues

B. Purpose of tongues
The purpose of speaking in tongues—indeed, the purpose of all gifts of the Spirit—is the building up of the body of Christ.

II. GIFTS OF THE SPIRIT: BUILDING CHRIST'S CHURCH

A. Gifts as applied to offices may be divided into "natural" and "unnatural"

B. Both "natural" and "unnatural" gifts are given for some function
ILLUSTRATION: Physician has gift of physical healing as well as faith healer

C. Gifts are most often mundane
ILLUSTRATION: Physical sight—assistance to a blind person

D. All gifts, "natural" or "unnatural," are for building up the body of Christ

III. BUILDING CHRIST'S CHURCH: STRENGTHENING THE BODY

A. Gifts are selectively given by the Spirit
ILLUSTRATION: Revivals in Brazil, U.S. universities, Korea

B. We are to use those gifts that build up the body
ILLUSTRATION: Parable of the tool crib

CONCLUSION: The Holy Spirit does not bestow gifts on believers as grandparents shower presents on their grandchildren. The Spirit gives to us the gifts we need and can use. Let us therefore seek those gifts that are needed in the church where we serve. And in the power of the Spirit, let us use those gifts for the strengthening of the body of Christ.

Arrangement. Presentation of a theme or idea from its simplest statement to its most complex is a favorite approach in teaching and may be used to advantage in preaching as well. It is especially suited to consideration of controversial issues such as this one, as the initial, simple treatment puts the subject on the table and the remainder of the sermon places it in proper context. The arrangement may also be reversed, with the reasoning moving from complex to simple.

Exegetical Note. The Corinthian church was known for its excesses. Paul found it necessary to admonish the Corinthians for going overboard in the practice of the gifts of the Spirit. It is significant that in his listing there is no distinction between what we would call "natural" gifts or abilities—teaching, helping, administration—and those we would identify as "unnatural" or even "supernatural"—miracle-working, prophecy, healing, speaking in tongues. According to the apostle, all gifts are given by the Spirit to be used for the building of the church.

Design. The introduction tells the story of a seminary senior caught in a bind. In this way, from the very beginning, the issue is lifted from the abstract and made personal. The sermon moves to a survey of erroneous attitudes because, much like repentance in Jonah 3, the subject needs to have the underbrush cleared away before the good seed is planted. The concluding parable of the tool crib, explained on page 83, is an extended allegory on the need for workers to have tools (gifts) appropriate to their tasks.

Thesis. The Third Person of the Trinity is the Spirit of order and harmony, not of discord. The tensions we see in the church over issues of the work of the Spirit show that our immaturity matches that of the Corinthians. When we understand how the Holy Spirit provides gifts for a variety of people in a multitude of settings all for the purpose of building the church, we gain a better appreciation not only of the Spirit but also of each other.

The Components of a Sermon

The Introduction or Question

Arousing Interest. The critical sixty seconds in a sermon are the first sixty seconds. The prayer for illumination has been delivered, the Scripture has been read, and the people wait expectantly. As the appetizer (clams casino) whets the appetite for the entrée (beef Wellington), so should the introduction sharpen the interest of the congregation for what follows. The preacher who arouses curiosity, stimulates the imagination, pricks the conscience, or develops a sense of intrigue in this critical first minute will in most cases have an attentive congregation for the entire sermon. Once the interest of the congregation is lost, however, it is almost impossible to retrieve it. Not all sermons have the same degree of potential interest. A sermon on sex may be of somewhat greater interest than, say, one on tithing, but both are subjects that need to be addressed from the pulpit. It is the preacher's responsibility from the first sentence to create a sense of expectancy so that the remainder of the sermon may be heard and acted upon.

Revealing the Question. The introduction that discloses the thesis or assertion of the sermon reveals too much. The purpose of the introduction is to raise the question that the assertion will answer. It is appropriate that the beginning create a certain level of tension in the hearer: a question in need of an answer, a problem without an immediate solution, a conflict left unresolved, opposing claims not reconciled. An effective introduction does not let the cat out of the bag. It entices the congregation into thinking and questioning with the preacher so that, together, pastor and people enter the body of the sermon (the assertion) to seek an answer from the Bible.

The sermon from 1 Corinthians 12, for example, begins with a seminarian caught on the horns of a dilemma. As the incident is revealed, the point of view of the questioner is deliberately left unstated. Nor does the incident indicate the position that will be developed, the assertion. The seminarians in the chapel, many of whom have faced or will soon face a similar interrogation, are left to identify with the student in the story. In making personal a complex theological issue and creating a mood of tension, sympathy, and identification, the introduction has accomplished its purpose. The congregation is now prepared to hear the assertion.

Beginning in the Present. A sermon should begin in the lives of the people and take them to the Word of God. In the great majority of cases, the introduction should be set in the present: an example, story, quotation, or some other contemporary expression of the question. A sermon that begins in the text (or, worse, in a background treatment of the context) runs the risk of losing the attention of the hearers, because they live not in the first century but in the twentieth. Strategically, the preacher needs to gain a hearing by demonstrating a concern for and knowledge of the life situation of the people. (More than one congregation has lamented that the pastor seems to live in the Bible.) When this important first step is taken, the preacher may move to the teaching of the text.

It would be entirely appropriate for an exegetical lecture on 1 Peter 2:1–10 to begin by establishing the authorship of the epistle, identifying textual problems, describing the literary genre, and detailing the nature of the churches addressed in Asia Minor. Such an approach from the pulpit would leave lay folk in the exegetical dust, however, so the sermon begins with a simple description of a contemporary phenomenon: people uncovering family histories in order to gain a sense of identity. In a typical congregation, many families would have already undertaken this search. With the mind of the congregation on the question of roots and identity, the preacher proceeds to the imagery of the text in the body of the sermon.

The Body or Assertion

Keeping It Simple. In a sermon of twenty minutes, the body will commonly occupy fourteen to sixteen minutes. The introduction and conclusion, given their brevity, can usually be composed without much consideration of structure. In order to develop the argument, maintain a smooth flow of ideas, and ensure a sense of symmetry in the major sections, it is best to outline the body of the sermon before the drafting process begins.

As most of us learned outlining in high school English classes with absolute rules (every subpoint *A* has to be accompanied by a *B*, no mixing of clauses and complete sentences, etc.), it is appropriate to remember that the preacher's outline will never see the light of day outside the study. The outline is not going to be submitted to anyone; it is the means to the end of a smooth, cogent, and persuasive finished sermon. The five sermon outlines in this chapter have either two or three major headings in the body. A two-part development is probably the most common, for it lends itself well to comparison-contrast types of treatment. Probably the maximum number of headings that can be addressed in twenty minutes is three, so if the preacher is working with four or more points, some consolidation is in order.

In the outline, clauses are to be preferred to full sentences, especially in the major headings. Briefer statements prevent the outline from becoming a semi-manuscript. Also, if the preacher takes the outline into the pulpit, it is far easier to look down and find a clause or a one- or two-word heading than to search for a complete sentence.

Making Application. The contemporary meaning should be stated as the sermon moves along rather than saved for the end. Recent seminary graduates may be prone to preaching academic-type sermons in which the first half develops the text and the second half applies the meaning to a life situation. (For the first ten minutes the preacher is saying, "I'm bright, I can do exegesis, I went to seminary." For the next ten minutes the message is, "I love you people, I'm your pastor.") Such a bifurcation not only divorces the text from the application but risks losing the congregation right at the beginning. It is a lazy preacher who expects people to carry the weight of the biblical meaning along to the conclusion in order to grasp the point of the sermon. The hardworking preacher does the integration of text and issue, past and present, exposition and application, and eases the burden of the listeners.

In the problem-solution sermon from Romans 8:18–25, the meaning of both futility and hope are developed in biblical time and terminology and brought forward to the present. Exposition and application should be seen not as separate entities but as strands of a cable intertwined and stretching through the entire message. The congregation, in hearing the sermon, should have a sense of never being far from the text or the contemporary setting.

Maintaining Uniformity. The flow of a sermon is made smoother by following an outline that is consistent not only in faithfulness to the theme but also in its use of tense, mood, number, and voice. Once again, the purpose of constructing a uniform arrangement is not so the lay people can go home with a classic outline but so the sermon will maintain the same tone all the way through. If there are three major headings, for example, with one in the indicative mood, the second in the imperative, and the third in the interrogative, the body (assertion) begins with a statement, moves on to a command, and ends with a question. Such mood changes are likely to cause confusion. The same can be said of a sermon where major structure includes verbs in both passive and active voice, mixtures of past, present, and future tenses, and combinations of singular and plural. When preparation reaches the manuscript stage, the writing is far more easily done when uniformity has been maintained in the outline.

The Conclusion or Invitation

Stressing Action. The conclusion needs to answer the question "So what?" Now that the people have heard the reading of the Scripture, the raising of a question from their life experience, and the answering assertion from the text, what are they to do? Is the appropriate response a deepening of faith? A renewed commitment? Changed behavior? Modified attitudes? If the preacher has no clear sense of appropriate action at the finish of the sermon, then neither will the congregation.

The conclusion is the final opportunity to apply the meaning of the text. Accordingly, if an illustration or story is employed it should be motivational in nature. The final minute is not the time for summarizing the content of the sermon or a last chance to restate the teaching of the Scripture. A strong conclusion builds on the body and sends people into the world to act on what they have heard and experienced in the preaching of the Word.

Integrating the Content. A proper conclusion flows naturally out of the body and ends the sermon with emphasis and power. The conclusion should contain no new ideas or themes but motivate the congregation to act on what has already been presented. The final minute or two is the last opportunity the preacher has to nail down the behavioral implications of the text as it relates to the issue of the sermon. Therefore, the focus needs to be restricted, not enlarged.

It is not unusual to hear the edge of many sermon conclusions blunted by such trite lead-ins as "Finally" or "In conclusion" or "Just let me add. . . ." These apologetic leads not only rob the conclusion of its power but also suggest to the hearers that the sermon is over. Such lines may be called hymnal-pullers, for the moment the preacher says "And finally," the sound of fabric scraping over hardwood racks can be heard throughout the sanctuary. People who are thumbing their way through the pages to the hymn are going to miss the climax of the sermon.

Ensuring Brevity. The conclusion should be brief, probably not more than two minutes. If the body is properly constructed, the progression of ideas will build to a logical and emotional finale. A belabored conclusion is at best superfluous and at worst counterproductive. (Nothing is quite so annoying as a salesperson who continues the pitch even after we've decided to buy the product.) In many sermons a brief paragraph will be sufficient to reinforce the motivational emphasis coming out of the body. Overdrawn, overblown, and overly long conclusions are usually the preacher's compensation for a poorly structured and developed sermon.

5

Making the Sermon Memorable

It is not uncommon for beginning preachers to wrestle with the proper use of stories, anecdotes, and quotations to support the thesis of the sermon and impress it upon the minds of the hearers. Not a few pastors, after listening to master storytellers spin their magic in the pulpit, despair of ever being able to use illustrations effectively. Frustration leads to self-doubt, which gives rise to an endless series of questions: Where can I find good illustrations? How do I work the story into the sermon? Should I make the point before the example or after? Am I using too many stories, or too few?

In some quarters the sermon illustration has fallen on hard times. Those who believe the primary purpose of the sermon is to teach the meaning of the text have little patience with extrabiblical material, particularly when that material appeals more to the emotions than to reason. Others argue that if the meaning of the message is perfectly clear in the first telling, there is no need for illustration. Still others have quite properly reacted against "story preachers," many of whom have gained fame, influence, and even wealth by trading on their ability to tell stories when a critical dissection of their work reveals little of biblical or theological substance.

In assessing the propriety of support material in the sermon, we might well heed the words not of a professional who preaches sermons but of a lay person who hears them. Vincent Drayne, a public relations executive, offers this wisdom:

> In my church, two different kinds of quotations from the Scriptures are read. One is called the epistle and the other the gospel.
>
> The epistles—well, you know what the epistles are—letters from the apostles to their brethren warning them against sin and urging them to do good. They are, in a way, little sermonettes which most of us need. But they are abstractions.
>
> But the gospels, now—they are stories. Nothing abstract about them. They start out like stories. Any time an opening sentence begins with words like these: "Now in the fifteenth year of the reign of Tiberius Caesar. . . ." you know something is going to happen. And that is true of leads like, "Now at that time, it came to pass . . . ," or "At that time, when it was late that same day. . . ."
>
> Most people can't remember much from the epistles. Everyone remembers the gospels. That taught me a great lesson. If I had my way, every speech would be a succession of stories. As it is, I go to a great deal of trouble hunting actual examples to illustrate the points I make.

The insightful incident, the sharp quotation, or the meaningful story, well related, integrated, and applied, can be the preacher's best friend. If such material is to have its desired effect, it must be chosen and used with considerable care.

Functions of Sermon Illustrations

Clarity. The primary function of the illustration is to clarify. "To illustrate" means to cast light on, and if the item employed fails to shed light on the thesis of the sermon, it has not accomplished its purpose. The illustration that is unclear or self-serving or that calls attention to itself or is not relevant to the point actually obscures the message.

Human Interest. Stories usually involve people, and because the teaching of the Bible is often couched in abstract terms, a specific incident or situation related in the sermon will make personal and concrete the abstract lessons of the Scriptures. When the hearers can identify with the persons in the story, they are better able to grasp the significance of the text.

Instruction. There is literally no limit to the amount of material that can be impressed upon the consciousness of a congregation by means of the illustration. In the annals of church history and missions, for example, there is a wealth of material that allows the preacher to draw parallels between the church and its ministry in our time and place and the life of God's people in other times and other lands. Many illustrations can serve two purposes, illumination and instruction.

Relief. As any student in a lecture class knows, concentrated listening is hard work. A well-placed story allows the congregation to relax and be carried along by the illustration. Because it is almost impossible for people to resist being drawn into a story, the illustration is a superb device for reviving the attention of a congregation when minds begin to wander.

Repetition. The Hebrews often used parallelism to repeat a message and reinforce its meaning without tiring the hearer or reader. With adroit use of support material, the preacher can accomplish the same purpose. A contemporary example of the lesson taught by the text not only will make the meaning personal, and bring it to the present, but will also serve as a retelling, in a new and interesting setting, of the same message.

Breaking Down Resistance. One of the most important uses of stories and quotations is to short-circuit emotional reaction. When you are advancing ideas that may receive a less-than-receptive hearing or even be met with resistance, an illustration can provide an indirect lead-in that is more likely to gain a fair hearing than a more frontal, didactic approach. Quotations from people or sources respected by the congregation can be used to great advantage in supporting viewpoints that might not be readily accepted if stated entirely as the preacher's own. It's always nice to have an expert on your side.

Purposes of Sermon Illustrations

Although many types and categories of stories, examples, and quotations could be listed, the essential purposes of sermon illustrations are only two in number: *explanation* and *motivation.*

Explanation

An Arabian proverb says that a good speech "turns the ears into eyes." The light from an illustration allows the congregation to "see" what is being said. The informative or explanatory illustration clarifies or amplifies a particular aspect of the teaching of the text or the application thereof. Because the explanatory illustration provides information, it is, in a sense, a teaching device: the preacher states a principle from the text, provides contemporary meaning, and confirms the argument with an example.

In the sermon from 1 Corinthians 12 in chapter 4, the point is made that the gifts of the Spirit may appear in what we would term "natural" or "unnatural" guise. No matter what the appearance, however, all such gifts are from the Spirit. In order to explain and clarify, a physician who is also an ordained minister is quoted. "I have the gift of healing," he says. "In my exercise of that gift I use surgery, medicines, and therapy. The faith healer uses anointing with oil and the laying on of hands. We both have the gift of healing; we just go about using it in different ways."

All healing is of God, but a common misconception is that all those who possess the gift use the techniques of the faith healer. The quotation from a practitioner of the healing arts reinforces the point that the great majority of those who exercise the gift do so in the mundane practice of medicine rather than in the more spectacular work of the faith healer. The working of the Holy Spirit is far more often seen in the ordinary than in the extraordinary.

Motivation

While the explanatory illustration informs and appeals primarily to the intellect, the motivational illustration stresses action and is directed to the will. As such, the story or quotation intended to drive the hearer to action will usually appear later in the message. A general rule of thumb is that explanatory material should be used earlier in the sermon, to prepare for the motivational content coming at the conclusion. Informational data prepare people for the call to action. If the preacher is still explaining and informing at the close of the sermon, it is not likely that the congregation will be motivated. On the other hand, if the sermon begins on a hortatory note without an informational base, the people will have little sense as to how, why, or to what they are being urged to move.

In the 1 Corinthians 12 sermon, a parable is used to close the third major point and lead in to the conclusion. The parable describes a tool crib in the center of a great construction project. Every morning the whistle blows and the workers line up to receive their implements from the tool boss before beginning their labor. One day the carpenter refused his hammer and saw and grabbed a wire cutter. The plumber spurned his blowtorch in favor of a pickax. The ironworker took a bulldozer instead of his welding gear. The electrician decided to take a jackhammer. Chaos reigned on the project, and work ground to a halt. At last the workers returned to the tool boss—the carpenter for his hammer and saw, the plumber for his blowtorch, the ironworker for his welding tanks, the electrician for his wire cutter and needle-nose pliers. Once again the sounds of progress filled the air, and the project moved toward completion. And the meaning of the parable? The construction job is the church, the workers are the members, the tool boss is the Holy Spirit, and the tools are the gifts of the Spirit. When Christians try to appropriate inappropriate gifts, there is chaos in the church. We are instead to seek and use those gifts the Spirit sees fit to give us.

Sources of Sermon Illustrations

The material available for use in sermons is limitless. Almost anything the preacher sees, hears, senses, or experiences can be used to make a point. Lay people often ask how long it takes to prepare a sermon, but this is an impossible question to answer because much material is discovered in such nonsermonic activities as reading the newspaper, riding the subway, going to the movies, or taking the kids to the zoo. The busy pastor of necessity develops a homiletical mind and becomes sensitized to the sermonic potential of a wide range of perceptions and experiences.

The great novelist, poet, or playwright is not a person who creates highly unusual characters and events but, rather, one who finds deep meaning and insight in the everyday situations of life. So too with the effective preacher. The key to the discovery and use of powerful support data is not possession of a vivid imagination that dreams up incredible new stories but the development of a keen and purposeful vision of the ordinary. A reading of Hebrew apocalyptic literature reveals that the ancient Jews were capable of great flights of imagination, but when Jesus preached to the people he drew from the everyday world to make his meaning clear: the weather, news events, cooking, planting, changing seasons, housecleaning, business, coinage, family relations, sewing.

Reading

Endless hours spent squinting at small print in journals and reference books come with the pastoral territory, but the parish preacher needs to be a person who reads beyond the theological and professional. For most of us, reading widely requires a conscious effort, but the busy pastor who is willing to follow a reading program beyond the essential will discover an actual saving of time in gathering sermon data, for news events, incidents, and quotations will present themselves.

Karl Barth described the preacher as a person with the Bible in one hand and a newspaper in the other. Daily papers and a news/opinion magazine are essential reading. The pastor should also be exposed to what the congregation is reading: in a rural parish, a farm journal; in a suburban commuter locale, a business publication; in youth ministry, a teen magazine; in campus ministry, the local alternative papers. A variety of books should grace the pastor's coffee table: history, fiction, biography, social commentary, humor. Such offerings need not be a significant drain on the family budget, for best-sellers are now appearing in paperback while still on the charts. Also, the pastor can order books for the church library and read them before they go on the shelves—at no personal expense.

The one type of book that has no place in the study, manse, parsonage, or rectory is a volume of sermon illustrations. If the Supreme Court ever wished to rid the nation of publications with no redeeming social value, it would begin with a ban on all such books. Tediously indexed by subject (forgiveness, grace, heaven, mortality, stewardship), such volumes are paper mausoleums of Victorian religiosity, stories repeated and embellished so often over the years that they have come to us as half-truths, partial truths, and just plain untruths designed to put the most attentive congregation to sleep. The larger specimens may serve as doorstops, but no other useful purpose can be imagined.

Observations

What sets outstanding critics, writers, commentators, and even preachers apart from those of lesser rank is their ability to see what others miss. A treasure trove of sermon fodder, free for the observing, presents itself as the pastor travels, shops, sits in meetings, drives a car, plays golf, or generally goes about the routine business of life. The preacher must be a student of human behavior as well as a student of the Word. The theater, television, popular music, and the cinema are obvious sources. The more perceptive pastor will remain alert during commercials while watching television. Advertisers paying six figures for thirty seconds of air time make extensive use of motivational research, and the commercial spot can tell us much about the attitudes, needs, values, fears, and aspirations of the audience to whom it is directed.

Experience

All sermons come to the hearers out of the preacher's life. (When a novelist was asked recently if his work was autobiographical, he replied enigmatically, "I'm writing from my imagination—but I know my imagination.") The personality of the preacher is an integral part of the sermon. There is, however, a school of thought that contends that the pastor should not make overt use of his or her own experience. Many eminent preachers of earlier generations adhered to this dictum and never referred to themselves from the pulpit. Without going to the opposite extreme, in which the sermon becomes an egotistical monologue or therapy session, a preacher who makes judicious use of personal experience brings strength and vitality to the message and, through it, comfort and edification to the lay people. A simple but workable rule as a check against overuse of experience is a limit of one personal example per sermon.

Principles for Using Sermon Illustrations

Relation. The example or quotation should be related directly to the point being made. It matters not at all whether the illustration precedes or follows the argument. The approach may be deductive, with the point stated first and then illustrated, or inductive, with the illustration related first and the point made from it. Whichever approach is chosen, the relationship of principle and example needs to be made clear.

Integration. In order to maintain a smooth sermonic flow, some attention should be given to the insertion of illustrative material. Generally, a brief pause and a change of expression is sufficient to alert the congregation to a change of mood or emphasis. Examples and illustrations lose their power if introduced with "A good illustration of this is . . . ," which gives the impression that the preacher is trying to sell his or her own story. Such an announcement also slows the pace of the sermon. No comedian introduces gags by saying, "Here's a great joke about a used-car salesman. . . ." Interest will be lost if the pace is not maintained. Congregations can recognize illustrations without being told what they are.

Proximity. Examples selected for inclusion in the sermon should be close to the congregation in time, place, interest, and, most important, acceptance. Pastor A might draw an illustration from an R-rated movie, while Pastor B's flock would be mortified if they thought their minister saw such stuff. Quotations can be tricky, as a perfectly good citation may come from a problematic source. In Parish X a quotation from an agency or officer of the World Council of Churches can be used to positive effect, but the worshipers in Parish Y would react negatively to any mention of the WCC. Sometimes perfectly valid material will have to be struck from the sermon because the source will not be acceptable to the congregation, and therefore the material will not have a fair hearing.

Concreteness. Nothing injects life into a story better than hard details. When the preacher can cite specific dates ("in 1944" rather than "during World War II"), actual places ("on the parade ground at the Sachsenhausen concentration camp" not "in a Nazi prison camp"), and real people ("Pastor Martin Niemoeller," as opposed to "a German pastor"), the congregation knows it is hearing a story chosen and crafted with purpose and care. This is not to argue that only factual or historical data may be used. Indeed, some of our most powerful sermonic images come from fairy tales, novels, and comic strips, to name but three sources of fiction. A story from either history or fiction will have much greater interest and impact if told accurately, thoroughly, and with details in place.

Timeliness. Whatever the occasion, the sermon is enhanced by the inclusion of appropriate illustrations and quotations for that day or season. For example, a citation from the life or work of Martin Luther will have greater impact on Reformation Sunday than on other dates. The marking of a church anniversary is the time to rummage through records and archives for a suitable story. Each day, season, observance, or special occasion creates in the congregation a predisposition or expectancy that should be exploited by the preacher.

Economy. If illustrations are to have maximum effect, they must be used sparingly. Two or more examples in sequence usually mean that the preacher is illustrating the illustrations.

One strong example is always to be preferred over several weak ones, just as a single good excuse for late submission of a term paper will generally gain mercy, while a recitation of eight lame alibis will not. Each supporting item should have a clearly thought out purpose in the sermon.

Pitfalls of Sermon Illustrations

Old Preacher's Stories. The oral equivalent of the calcified item from a book of sermon illustrations is the story that has passed from preacher to preacher until its origins and veracity defy discovery. The sure sign that such an old chestnut is being foisted onto a hapless congregation is the lead-in "The story is told. . . ." An illustration of such uncertain parentage usually adds little to the sermon and reflects badly on the preacher.

Hypothetical Stories. When the preacher waxes creative, his or her energies should be poured into the well-crafted parable or fable. The hypothetical example dashed off with "Let's assume for the moment . . ." gives the sermon an air of improbability. Stories of this type may create the impression that the preacher is making up the sermon as he or she goes along.

Pastoral Counseling References. One of the few absolutes in preaching is that there should be no stories told from the pulpit out of the pastor's counseling ministry. Even if the incident goes back many years to a previous parish hundreds of miles away, with names and details altered, listeners will perceive parallels (real and imagined) to persons in the church or community and say to themselves (and later to others), "I know who that is." Even if no inferences are drawn (and they invariably are), the preacher who relates counseling experiences will find that church members are reluctant to seek counsel from someone who is likely to turn their cases into sermon illustrations.

Family Stories. The pastor will constantly be aware of incidents centering on spouse and children that will fit perfectly into a sermon and illustrate a particular point. It is a wise and compassionate preacher who will resist the temptation to use the "perfect" story. The fishbowl existence of a clergy family is never easy, and there is little reason to compound the difficulty by compromising precious privacy from the pulpit. Psychiatrists who treat the families of celebrities report that when children are pushed into the public eye they often identify so completely with their famous parent(s) that they develop little or no identity of their own. This sad pattern has been repeated over and over again in the church. When the pastor deletes a superb domestic story from the Sunday message, the sermon may suffer but the family will prosper.

Inappropriate Self-Reference. The preacher's self-disclosures from the pulpit should reveal a balanced person. As we all have our moments of triumph and defeat, hope and despair, fulfillment and frustration, the material that relates to ourselves should disclose the range of experiences and emotions. If the pastor is the hero in all personal stories, doing the proper thing and speaking the right word at just the right time, the congregation will soon perceive an outsized ego. If, on the contrary, all such illustrations center on failure, the pastor will be viewed as a complete klutz. An occasional survey of past sermons with a view to maintaining balance in self-reference is a sound idea.

Name-Dropping. It is human nature to desire to enhance our own prestige by linking ourselves to someone more famous or accomplished. In the sermon, these efforts backfire almost immediately when the congregation senses that the purpose of a story is not to enhance understanding of the message but to prop up the stature of the preacher. Often stories will border on the dishonest, as with the preacher who begins, "When I had lunch with the governor last Tuesday . . . ," when in fact the pastor was one of 687 clergy attending the annual State Council of Churches governor's luncheon. In many cases the impact of the story will actually be greater if the personal involvement of the preacher is omitted.

Jesus made extensive use of stories in his teaching. With a touch of hyperbole, Mark writes, "He did not speak to them without a parable" (Mark 4:34). Our Lord understood the lure of a story and its power to draw people into the message so that hearers become participants with the preacher. It is this capacity to involve the listener that makes the sermon illustration indispensable to the preacher.

6
Making the Meaning Clear

"Words, words, words, I'm so sick of words!" cried Liza Doolittle in *My Fair Lady*. If the truth were told, not a few lay people in our pews would sound the same lament. Nineteen centuries ago, Paul wrote to the Romans, "How are they to believe in him of whom they have never heard? And how are they to hear without a preacher?" (Rom. 10:14). The problem confronting today's pastor would boggle the mind of the apostle, for our people have not only heard, they have heard again and again and again. In gaining and holding a congregation, the edge of novelty enjoyed by Paul is long gone. Our first-century colleagues could holler for a hearing in the marketplace and with little effort attract a curious crowd ready and willing not only to hear but also to discuss the ideas presented. For our people, the most exciting truth in the world is an ancient message that has been heard many times over. If we are to gain and hold a hearing for an old and familiar message, we must state it with style, simplicity, and power.

Word Power

Simplicity

Unabridged dictionaries of the English language contain approximately 500,000 listings, and most people, by the time they reach adulthood, are able to recognize about 90,000 words. In everyday conversation, however, we ordinarily use a vocabulary of only 600 words. Each discipline has its own specialized language and jargon that could be added to the total, but the common working lexicon for twentieth-century English-speaking people is less than 1,000 words.

The task of the preacher is not to probe the limits of the unabridged dictionary in an effort to educate the congregation in the 500,000 words available to them. Nor should the preacher work the parameters of the 90,000 recognizable words. The effective preacher is the one who knows how to use the ordinary vocabulary of 600 words to articulate the gospel message clearly and succinctly.

In late 1960, when President-elect John F. Kennedy began preparing his inaugural address, he assigned speechwriters Theodore Sorensen and Richard Goodwin the task of studying Lincoln's second inaugural to determine what made it such an outstanding speech. When they had completed their analysis, Sorensen and Goodwin reported that the secret of Lincoln's power was that he never used two words where one would suffice and that he refused to use two- and three-syllable words where a one-syllable word would carry the meaning as well. Most church budgets and ministerial salaries preclude the retention of high-priced talent like Sorensen and Goodwin, but the realistic and practical lesson to be drawn from this example is free: power and clarity in all oral discourse, including preaching, stem from the intelligent and economical use of simple English.

Imagery

The power of language lies not in the words themselves but in the images the words evoke. A generation ago it was popular to argue that in the global village the spoken word was passé—the visual was in and the verbal was out. We were warned that if the church wanted to keep pace, or even survive in a media society, the sermon would have to be discarded in favor of dance, drama, film, and multimedia presentations. Pulpits and lecterns would have to be removed from our chancels, the doomsayers told us, and replaced by stages, screens, strobe lights, and cathode-ray tubes. While some ministerial and theological types rallied to the electronic banner, the lay people who inhabit our pews did not salute it. The laity was not down on preaching per se, only on preaching that failed to address the faithful in their life situations and help them in living the Christian life.

Before leaving those of the Woodstock generation who criticized the spoken word, let it be said that they had a valid point: the visual is inherently more powerful than verbal. What the critics failed to understand, however, is the tremendous power contained in words that reach into our minds and unlock the visual images, associations, and memories we carry with us every day of our lives. In most cases, the shortest and most economical route to the visual inventory in the mind of the receiver is by the spoken word.

An advertisement for the American Broadcasting Company radio network news department has challenged the ancient axiom that a picture is of greater value than words:

> One picture worth a thousand words? You give me 1,000 words and I'll take the Lord's Prayer, the Twenty-Third Psalm, the Hippocratic Oath, a sonnet by Shakespeare, the Preamble to the Constitution, Lincoln's Gettysburg Address, and I'd still have enough words left over for just about all of the Boy Scout oath. And I wouldn't trade you for any picture on earth.

The reason the person stuck with the picture would get the short end of the bargain is that the mere mention of each literary item on the list triggers a mental re-creation of dozens of pictures. There are appeals to religious and spiritual values, health, love, romance, patriotism, history, valor, citizenship, justice, and tradition. Rather than maintaining possession of a single painting, sketch, or photograph, the person armed with a command of language is able to produce hundreds and even thousands of pictures.

Verbal discourse is able to go beyond the graphic, because not only can images be evoked and reproduced but concepts can be developed as well. The visual media, particularly television, are well suited to depicting objects but ill equipped to deal with ideas. It is not an accident, therefore, that television preachers feature soaring buildings, splashing fountains, photogenic singers, well-coiffed family members, and the flashiest smiles cosmetic dentistry can buy. Serious presentations of theological verities are seldom if ever heard or seen, for the small screen in the living room presents things well but is not at all suited to the presentation of ideas.

Word Recognition

New Vocabulary

Human language is a dynamic rather than a static institution. Definitions and usages are constantly changing; words, expressions, and patterns of speech become obsolete and are dropped, only to be replaced by newer vocabulary and constructions. It has always been thus, but our media society has accelerated the process to a remarkable degree.

While words and expressions come into the language from all manner of sources, it seems that at any given period of time there is one popular and influential institution or discipline that forces its specialized vocabulary (or jargon) into common speech. A generation ago, sociology was a new and hot discipline. Vance Packard, David Riesman, and Marshall McLuhan wrote best-sellers and saw and heard their verbal coin gain acceptance in both written and spoken discourse: hidden persuaders, status-seeker, exurbanite, organization man, mass culture, lonely crowd, acoustic space, hot and cool media, global village. Ours is a technological generation, and new terminology is coming into use from the computer field every few microseconds: memory bank, transponder, systems overload, bits, bytes, chips, software/hardware, disk drive, and on and on.

New Meanings

Not only are we constantly confronted by new words and expressions, but old terms take on new and sometimes unexpected meanings. There may be temporary confusion as a new connotation replaces an older denotation. Words are often cheapened by misuse or overuse. Our perception of the word "important," for example, is altered when a television program is interrupted by a smooth baritone voice saying, "We pause now for these important messages." And what are the "important" messages? A string of commercials for a toothpaste, a fabric softener, a beer, and a radial tire. While the messages are certainly important to the sponsors, they are an annoying intrusion to the viewer. The word "important" becomes a casualty of improper usage. (A similar fate has befallen "adult": there is nothing quite so juvenile as "adult" movies and magazines.)

In the church we have had some venerable and valuable words all but taken away from us. When the news media speak of born-again supply-side economists, evangelical cult leaders, charismatic political candidates, and fundamentalist Shiite Muslims, and automobile manufacturers urge us to "catch the spirit" or buy a certain sedan because it is "something to believe in," the time has come for us to exercise some discretion in our use of old terminology. We who make our livings with language are well advised to be sensitive to changes in word perception and understanding.

One of the most basic principles of language is that the meanings of words are vested in the people who use them rather than in the words themselves. As an exercise, we might throw out the word "draft" at a party. The meaning? To the engineer, it is a technical drawing; to the young university student, it is involuntary military conscription; to the writer, it is a copy of a work in progress; to the beer drinker, it is a favorite beverage; to the farmer, it is an animal bred for pulling plows and wagons; to the poor resident of substandard housing, it is the chilling stream of air that blows all winter long; to the weekend sailor, it is the distance between the waterline and the keel; to the race-car driver, it is the partial vacuum created by a car at speed. The meaning is not in the word itself but in the people who hear it.

In preaching, therefore, it is the words in which people have already invested meaning that have power. Unknown and unfamiliar expressions do little to help the communication process.

There is an unfortunate tendency for beginning professionals in any field, beset as they are by rookie insecurity, to hide behind the barrier of official (and officious) vocabulary. Cub lawyers spout Latin in courthouse corridors, young interns recite medical-text definitions at hospital bedsides, and beginning preachers bless the faithful with seminary-speak (pericope, Hellenism, synoptic, kerygma, myth, historicism, apocalyptic, exegesis, Septuagint, gnostic). Veteran attorneys, physicians, and ministers are sufficiently secure in their chosen career roles that the protective armor of professional jargon can be discarded. However, there are congregations that view the coming of a newly minted pastor with some foreboding as they anticipate a few years of pulpit purgatory before sermons sound less like seminary table conversation and more like messages directed to lay people in lay language. Witness the lament of a laywoman serving on her church's pastoral search committee: "So far we've interviewed four enablers, two facilitators, and a vulnerable healer. Sometime soon I hope we talk to a pastor."

Writing for the Ear

There are preachers who counsel against the writing down of sermons. A sermon that has been written, they contend, lacks a sense of spark and originality and sounds like the oral presentation of a research paper. Granted that the manuscript process may (and often does) yield a dull sermon, when the preacher understands the difference between writing for the ear and writing for the eye, the scripting effort will actually enhance the oral style of the finished product. With an appreciation for spoken English, the preacher can write and then revise the sermon with a view toward eliminating words, expressions, and constructions that are more suited to written discourse.

Candidates for ordained ministry receive their training in the traditional academic setting, where they read journals, theologies, histories, and commentaries, all written in the proper academic style, so it is not surprising that when they create reports and papers they write in this same mode. And when they stand up to preach, this style often sounds forth from the pulpit, with or without the use of a manuscript. After four years of university study and three of theological study, the seminarian speaks term-paper English without self-consciousness. With a manuscript spread on the desk, however, the beginning preacher is able to edit out academic and technical language before delivering the sermon from the pulpit.

There are significant differences between the English we speak and the English we write. Some key characteristics of spoken English are as follows:

Fewer Words. In speaking, we use a restricted vocabulary. For variety and interest, the writer will employ a greater number of different words. The speaker has the advantage of multiplying the range of meaning of common English words many times over by the proper gestures, posture, facial expressions, and vocal inflection.

Shorter Words. In speaking, we use words of fewer syllables. Multisyllabic words are both difficult for hearers to understand and difficult for speakers to say. While contractions may not be used in many types of writing, they are perfectly acceptable in public address.

Good-Sounding Words. In speaking, we are concerned with how language sounds to the ear and quite unconcerned with how it appears on the page. Dramatic effects can be gained by the repetition of words and phrases that would quickly tire a reader.

Sensuous Words. In speaking, we should not only create visual images for the mind's eye but also employ words that appeal to other senses and sensations. The Bible was written in an oral age and is replete with sensuous expressions: the scroll offered Ezekiel is "as sweet as honey"; the Laodicean church is "lukewarm, and neither cold nor hot," and fit only to be spit out; the wise proverb says, "A soft answer turns away wrath"; Jesus uses the image of a woman in labor in his farewell to his disciples; Isaiah likens the Lord to "a shade from the heat."

Strong Nouns and Verbs. In a speech, adjectives and adverbs do more to complicate the presentation than to strengthen it.

Definite nouns and action verbs render modifying and qualifying words superfluous and permit lean, hard prose.

Indicative Mood. In preaching, we should utilize the indicative mood as much as possible and be sparing in our use of the imperative. There is something in human nature that resists commands. People are far more likely to respond positively to urging and encouraging than to demanding language.

First-Person Plural. In preaching, we should indicate our solidarity with the congregation in submission to the Word by employing "we"-language rather than "you"-language. The first-person plural helps avoid the almost inevitable distaste people feel when they sense they are being "preached at." When combined with the imperative mood, second-person wording can all but drive people out of the church. Strong messages receive a better hearing when phrased in the first-person plural indicative.

Inclusive Language. In preaching, it is our task to address all our people, not only those who are male. While there is much in grammar and tradition to support the view that "man," "mankind," and masculine pronouns are generic terms that include both sexes, the church has some obligation to place human sensitivity before grammatical and traditional considerations. It isn't difficult to substitute plural usage—they, them, their—for the masculine pronouns he, him, his. "Humanity" and "humankind" are preferred to "mankind," and "person" can be used in place of "man."

Ego Language. In preaching, we may dispense with the academic prohibitions against references to I, me, my, mine, and myself. Oral discourse without personal pronouns would sound strange indeed. To avoid the impression of egotism, however, it is good to limit ego words.

Example: "I Have a Dream," by Martin Luther King, Jr.

Some of the most vivid examples of oral style in preaching today are to be heard in black churches. The black community has learned eloquence the hard way. Until the middle of the last century, it was illegal to teach a slave to read and write. The slaves compensated by developing extremely sophisticated and effective patterns of oral communication. The elaborate imagery of black narratives, spirituals, work songs, and sermons often contained coded messages that white ears were not to understand. More than a century after emancipation, black preaching has maintained its unique oral character. While Caucasian preachers must shed the influences of German rationalism and academic literalism to begin to appreciate the joy of the spoken word, our black colleagues need only go back to their roots.

The Bible comes to us from oral societies. Writing in ancient times was a cumbersome task that fell to professionals who worked with clay tablets, animal skins, and papyrus. Not everyone was taught to read, and even those who were did little or no writing for themselves. Scribes were retained for writing wills and legal documents and copying precious manuscripts. As a result, the ancient Hebrews developed a keen ear for argument, narrative, and poetry, and the Scriptures are mostly a compilation of oral source material.

The style of the late Martin Luther King, Jr., as evidenced by the following paragraphs from his "I Have a Dream" address delivered in 1963, has a distinctly biblical ring to it. In fact, when King begins a quotation from Isaiah 40 with "I have a dream that one day every valley shall be exalted . . . ," the style of the biblical prophet is one with that of the black preacher.

I Have a Dream

I say to you today, my friends, though, even though we face the difficulties of today and tomorrow, I still have a dream. It is a dream deeply rooted in the American dream. I have a dream that one day this nation will rise up, live out the true meaning of its creed: "We hold these Truths to be self-evident, that all Men are created equal."

I have a dream that one day on the red hills of Georgia sons of former slaves and sons of former slave-owners will be able to sit down together at the table of brotherhood. I have a dream that one day even the state of Mississippi, a state sweltering with the heat of injustice, sweltering with the heat of oppression, will be transformed into an oasis of freedom and justice.

I have a dream that my four little children will one day live in a nation where they will not be judged by the color of their skin but by the content of their character. I have a dream . . .

I have a dream that one day in Alabama, with its vicious racists, with its governor having his lips dripping with the words of interposition and nullification, one day right there in Alabama, little black boys and little black girls will be able to join hands with little white boys and little white girls as sisters and brothers. I have a dream today . . .

I have a dream that one day every valley shall be exalted, every hill and mountain shall be made low. The rough places will be made plain, and the crooked places will be made straight. And the glory of the Lord shall be revealed, and all flesh shall see it together. This is our hope. This is the faith that I go back to the South with.

With this faith we will be able to hew out of the mountain of despair a stone of hope. With this faith we will be able to transform the jangling discords of our nation into a beautiful symphony of brotherhood. With this faith we will be able to work together . . . to stand up for freedom together, knowing that we will be free one day.

Style Commentary

Repetition. The title phrase "I have a dream" occurs nine times in this excerpt. An emotional appeal of considerable force is contained in the sentence "It is a dream deeply rooted in the American dream." King is reminding all who hear that black citizens have not shared that dream. The intoning of the four title syllables is a drumbeat reminder of that unfulfilled dream.

Vocabulary. The address is composed of one-, two-, and three-syllable words. Apart from the proper names Alabama and Mississippi, there is one four-syllable word, "difficulties," and a pair of five-syllable words, "interposition" and "nullification," chosen for polemical effect in reference to the governor of Alabama. The vocabulary throughout is common and easily understood.

Sensuous Words. The address abounds with appeals to the senses. Visual images predominate: "the table of brotherhood";

"an oasis of freedom and justice"; a nation in which children "will not be judged by the color of their skin but by the content of their character"; "Alabama . . . with its governor having his lips dripping with the words of interposition and nullification." References to children abound. (It is a foolish speaker who underestimates the persuasive power of images of children.) There is a tactile appeal in the description of black and white children, "able to join hands . . . as sisters and brothers." Speaking on a steamy August afternoon in Washington, D.C., King evoked the thermal sense of hot, humid weather when he referred to "Mississippi, a state sweltering with the heat of injustice, sweltering with the heat of oppression." There is a brief, well-phrased aural image in the exhortation to faith that "will be able to transform the jangling discords of our nation into a beautiful symphony of brotherhood."

Action Images. Two metaphors, one ordinary and the other quite extraordinary, link complex social movement to human action. The pedestrian image is that of a person arising, in the sentence "I have a dream that one day this nation will rise up, live out the true meaning of its creed." The metaphor that sings is one of labor in a massive task: "With this faith we will be able to hew out of the mountain of despair a stone of hope." King urges his hearers to visualize in the mountain of their despair a jewel in the rough that is hope.

First-Person Indicative. There are no imperatives employed here. A powerful argument does not require demanding and commanding language to be effective. Nor does King address his audience in the second person. "I" language is used to describe the dream. King shifts to the plural "we" language for exhortation to the task.

Not one of King's images is expanded and developed into an illustration in the traditional sermonic sense. The images are brief and to the point, most of them less than a single sentence. In them we experience the majesty of language and the ability of words to evoke pictures and feelings.

7
Preparing the Sermon

While this entire volume is concerned with the preparation of sermons, in this chapter we address the specific process of preparing a single sermon. An Epiphany sermon from John 2:1–11, Jesus at the marriage in Cana, is developed as an example. The pattern of study and creation described here is hardly *the* method of homiletical preparation; it is *a* method adapted from the writing of exegesis papers in seminary.

The reader is urged to study this working sequence as an encouragement to develop a personal pattern of homiletical labor that will make sermon preparation efficient, effective, satisfying, and, most important, fun. If the preacher does not find joy in the labor of biblical study and preaching, it is highly unlikely that the congregation will experience joy in the listening.

Principles for Use of Time

Early Beginning. Preparation should begin as early as possible. Some pastors are able to work a week ahead, finishing each sermon eight days or so before it is to be delivered, and this is an excellent schedule for those who can follow it. For those who cannot, the best time to undertake work on Sunday's sermon is

Monday morning; an early beginning is essential if the pastor is to avoid being caught in the crunch of time stemming from the frequent emergencies that are so much a fact of parish life. An early start not only allows more search time for data that will be a part of the sermon but also permits the subconscious power of the brain to do its essential labor of dredging ideas and bringing them to the conscious.

Specific Targeting. Effective preaching is born of concern for members of the congregation who will benefit most from the message—the destination of the Schramm model (Figure 2). As already noted, it is helpful to jot the initials of a few appropriate people on a scrap of paper. As the sermonic labor progresses, the pastor can glance at these initials from time to time and be reminded of the specific goal and purpose of the message.

Schedule Management. It is the pastor's responsibility to arrange and maintain a schedule that permits plenty of time for sermon preparation. For most people, the brain is fresh and alert in the morning hours, so this time should be reserved for study. Visitation, correspondence, administrative duties, appointments, and meetings can be left for afternoons and evenings.

Block Arrangement. Serious study and writing require large chunks of time, usually two hours or more at a stretch. Regrettably, countless dreary and unrealistic seminary lectureships on preaching have been delivered by ministers of mega churches who are able to read, reflect, and write thirty hours a week because they are shielded from congregation and community by a staff of associates in the parish and a battery of secretaries in the outer office. Beginning pastors in small parishes enjoy no such protection, but church people can be trained to respect the pastor's study time and to interrupt only for emergencies.

Gauging the Task. With a little experience the pastor will gain a sense of how much time must be devoted to the sermon. It has been popular in this generation to dismiss Harry Emerson Fosdick's advocacy of an hour in the study for every minute in the pulpit as excessive and unrealistic. Fosdick's standard remains a helpful and realistic one, however, as the labor of exegesis, organization, writing, and editing will not infrequently occupy twelve, fifteen, or even twenty hours. The preacher in all cases should take care not to underestimate the time required and be caught short.

Getting Ready for Work

Arranging Space

A typical pastor will spend upwards of 1,000 hours in the course of a year in preparing for sermons, lessons, weddings, funerals, and other presentations. In a forty-year ministry between ordination and Medicare, the totals are some 40,000 hours, or nearly five years behind the desk. The requisite labors will be accomplished with much greater efficiency if the working space is planned with some care. It is to the pastor's benefit to maintain a study separate from the office. A study is what the name implies: a place for research and writing, filled with books, journals, and files. The pastor's office is a room for administration, meetings, conferences, and counseling sessions. Because the office is where the minister meets the public, it is important that it be kept neat. A working study is a place where, when the pastor stops work for the day, the door can be closed on the stacks of books, open files, and scattered papers so typical of research in progress. The preacher may then return to the homiletical vineyard and resume work without having to rearrange tools hastily cleared away the evening before to create a tidy appearance for a board meeting or counseling session.

In most cases, the study will be better situated in the pastor's home rather than the church building. The study itself should be set up with good lighting, comfortable seating, adequate shelf space for books, and a large table area for spreading materials and writing.

Recording Information

At each working session it is helpful to have three tablets on the desk: two legal-size pads and a small notepad. One of the larger tablets is used for recording notes in the exegetical study of the text. This material is neatly organized under the title and section of each work consulted in the course of study. The second legal pad is kept beside the first and used as a stream-of-consciousness record of any and all thoughts regarding the sermon. In my study, I write the sermon text and trivia on the second pad. As work progresses, the record of research on the text is written on the exegesis tablet; ideas that come to mind for the sermon, including illustrations, a possible outline, quotations, an article or book to be consulted, are jotted down on the trivia pad.

In some ways, the small notepad is the most important of all. This tablet is for writing down important thoughts that come to mind but don't relate to the sermon: an appointment that must be kept that evening, a report to go out in the mail, an item to be picked up at the store. The brain is like a muscle, and when we exercise it, all manner of thoughts and ideas come into our heads, not all of them relevant to the subject of our work. If we try to retain a thought in our memories (the need to pick up the children at school at three fifteen to take them to soccer practice) while doing an exegesis of 1 Peter 2:18–25, we cannot give full mental attention to the epistle, and the kids are likely to be left standing on the curb. If we jot down these distracting thoughts, we can dismiss them from our minds and work with complete concentration. Most of us have enough difficulty doing serious exegetical study without handicapping ourselves by working at less than full brain capacity.

Beginning Each Session

It is a good habit to begin every study session with prayer and an oral reading of the sermon text. Good preaching springs from the prayer life of the preacher. The pastor should pray not only for illumination and discipline in the study of the Word but also for those who will hear the message. Specific prayer can be raised for those whose initials have been recorded and for whom the sermon is most appropriate. Reading the text aloud is an excellent study practice; the slower pace of reading often allows us to see meanings that escape us when we read silently. Also, the repeated oral readings will etch the text in our memories so that the passage will be memorized (or nearly so) when we stand to read it on Sunday morning.

Exegetical Study

It is hardly the intent of this section to develop a comprehensive treatment of biblical exegesis. The reader is referred to the work of Douglas Stuart, *Old Testament Exegesis: A Primer for Students and Pastors,* and Gordon D. Fee, *New Testament Exegesis: A Handbook for Students and Pastors,* as valuable, readable, and remarkably thorough brief treatments of the subject.

The assumption underlying this survey description is that biblical study for the sermon differs considerably from study done for exegesis papers. In theological school, the student in a Bible course chooses a pericope (e.g., Matt. 18:21–35) and devotes an entire term of ten to sixteen weeks to the production of a paper. In the parish three years later, the same student, now a rookie pastor, will in one week's time not only have to exegete the pericope for the sermon but also prepare a Bible study from Genesis 32; a confirmation class lesson on Holy Communion drawing from Matthew 26, Mark 14, Luke 22, John 13, and 1 Corinthians 11; a funeral sermon from Isaiah 40; and a wedding meditation from Colossians 3. Faced with demands on time that every parish generates, the harried pastor who must complete four or five biblical preparations a week looks back with bemused incredulity at the three months given to the exegesis and exposition of a single text in seminary.

It is therefore important that the pastor learn to do responsible and respectable exegesis for a sermon in four to five hours' time. Such rapid study need not be superficial if the preacher keeps the heart of a student and maintains basic language and exegetical skills.

If the work is begun at the very beginning of the week, the exegetical foundation for the sermon can be completed by Monday afternoon, leaving the remaining mornings free for completion of the sermon and other biblical preparations. A good rule of thumb is to consider the sermon one third complete when the exegesis is done. That is, the bare exegesis is to a sermon what the assembled ingredients are to a cake: after the milk, eggs, sugar, flour, shortening, baking powder, butter, vanilla, and chocolate have been assembled, the work of measuring, sifting, blending, mixing, baking, and decorating begins. When the preacher has finished the hard work of exegesis, there remains the hard work of organizing, writing, editing, and polishing. Indeed, many preachers have discovered that exegetical study is the easy part of sermon preparation.

Step 1: Reading the Text and Context

The study begins with reading from the version of the English Bible to be read in worship. It is a good habit to reread several times both the text itself and the chapters preceding and following, to gain a sense of the setting of the passage. Other translations may be consulted as well.

John 2:1–11. A survey reading of the beginning chapters of the Gospel of John places our text between the familiar prologue on the Word (1:1–18) and Jesus' conversation with Nicodemus (3:1–21). More immediately, the events in Cana are bracketed by the call of four disciples and the cleansing of the temple, which John places at the beginning of Jesus' ministry as opposed to the synoptic placement preceding the passion.

Step 2: Textual Study

Using the Hebrew Bible or the Greek New Testament, we establish the text. Quality translations of the English Bible are based on solid manuscript tradition and excellent scholarship, and the overwhelming majority of textual judgments made by the preacher will follow established readings. Only questions or problems in the text crucial to its meaning need be resolved; other variants that have scholarly interest may be left for the experts.

John 2:1–11. The most significant textual problem occurs in verse 3, where a later copyist seems to have added a gloss indicating that the wedding guests had no more wine to drink because the wine had all been consumed. The weight of manuscript tradition favors exclusion of this gloss, but the meaning of the pericope is unaffected in either case.

Step 3: Language Study

Blessed is the pastor who maintains a sufficient level of language skill to be able to translate from the original (and blessed is the congregation served by such a pastor). Because the preacher works under severe time constraints and is not producing a translation to endure for the ages, every aid and shortcut available can be put to use in translating. Whether a full translation is made or not, consult word studies and grammars for important words, constructions, and grammatical considerations.

John 2:1–11. Key words and phrases include the following:

A marriage (v. 1): A marriage festival including dinners and entertainment that may have lasted for a week.

Woman (v. 4): An affectionate form of address carrying no connotation of disrespect.

What have you to do with me? (v. 4): A gentle but firm assertion of independence.

Stone jars (v. 6): Actually, water pots or basins made from stone for ritual cleansing.

Steward of the feast (v. 9): Literally, the chief of the banquet hall. This person was usually a trusted servant or family friend who oversaw arrangements for the festival, including food, drink, and entertainment.

His disciples believed in him (v. 11): As a consequence of the miracle, Jesus' newly called disciples grasped his glory and believed. The first recorded instance of belief in Jesus.

Step 4: Theological Study

Volumes of biblical theology, be they Old or New Testament or theologies of particular books or authors, will place the sermon Scripture in theological context. Exegetical work in sermon preparation, limited as it is to specific texts, shows a greater kinship to biblical theology than to systematics. This is not to say that systematic theology does not address the homiletical task—quite the contrary—but in preparing sermons the sharper focus of the biblical theologian is of more immediate benefit than the broader view of the dogmatician. The preacher is more likely to read systematic theology in preparation for a series of sermons on doctrinal themes than for a single message.

John 2:1–11. In recording Jesus' attendance at the marriage in Cana, John draws a contrast between our Lord and his disciples and John the Baptist and his followers. In addition, the interplay of light and darkness, so essential to the Fourth Gospel, is seen in the context of chapter 2: at the very beginning of our Lord's ministry, the account of the wedding festival is followed immediately by the driving of the money changers from the temple. Unlike the Synoptic Evangelists, John places the cleansing in the first Passover of Jesus' ministry rather than in the third. John also uses the theme of seeing and believing as bookends for the Gospel: the disciples see and believe in Cana, and in 20:29, the original conclusion of the Gospel, Jesus says to Thomas, "Have you believed because you have seen me? Blessed are those who have not seen and yet believe." Prominent in John as well is the use of water for both purification and satisfaction of thirst.

Step 5: Historical and Factual Study

The tools in this stage of preparation include dictionaries of theology and the Bible, encyclopedias, atlases, and specialized reference works on particular portions of the Bible: for example, a history of Israel, a volume on Hebrew poetry, or a life of Jesus. The preacher works from the biblical indexes, checking listings of the sermon Scripture or consulting articles under significant people, places, events, objects, or customs appearing in the text.

John 2:1–11. Consulting entries according to the text as well as items under the headings Cana of Galilee, Marriage, Mary the mother of Jesus, Purification, and Weddings, the preacher gathers a wealth of material. Maidens were customarily married on Wednesdays, thus the "third day" reference in verse 1; Mary was present in Cana before Jesus, thus the marriage probably involved family friends; wedding guests often fasted and confessed sins before attending a marriage, thus a mixture of the solemn and the celebratory; the large, stone, ritual cleansing basins were conveniently placed for use by the guests, thus the miracle of turning water to wine would have been obvious to all.

Step 6: Interpretive Study

Significant by omission in our discussion so far is any mention of commentaries. This oversight is deliberate, for the preacher who reads and studies the Scripture textually, linguistically, theologically, and historically will achieve the satisfaction of developing her or his own interpretation of the passage. The pastor who begins study by reading the text and opening a commentary short-circuits the creative process. When steps 1 through 5 are followed, the preacher is in effect developing a personal commentary on the text—one that will have far greater meaning than the work of a biblical scholar, no matter how eminent, consulted at the beginning of the process.

John 2:1–11. Events at the beginning of the Gospel are set out with sufficient clarity that a chronology is possible. Working back from the marriage on Wednesday, it would seem that John the Baptist was questioned by the priests and Levites on the preceding Thursday (1:19–28), that Jesus returned from the wilderness and was proclaimed the Lamb of God by John and called Andrew and Peter as disciples on Friday (1:29–42); that Jesus called Philip and Nathanael on Saturday (1:43–51); that Jesus journeyed to Galilee and possibly called the remaining disciples on Sunday (2:1–2). This six-day period of full activity at Passover time marks the opening of Jesus' ministry as the six days of the Passion at the same season three years later marks the close. The contrast between Jesus and the ascetic John the Baptist is first established in our Lord's Son of man declaration to Nathanael in 1:51 and confirmed by attendance at the wedding. Some commentators find significance in the six water jars because six is one less than the complete number seven. A similar numerological point could be made regarding the six-day period in which this action takes place, although John does not specifically designate six days.

The notes shown in this section are not intended to stand as a complete or systematic exegesis of John 2:1–11, but they do indicate the types of data derived from each step of research. At the conclusion, the preacher may have from five to eight pages of exegetical notes and another two or three pages of sermon ideas.

Organizing the Material

With the completion of the exegetical research, the basic biblical components of the sermon have been assembled. In keeping the second trivia tablet at hand and jotting ideas, approaches, sources, and associations while recording the more formal biblical data, the preacher now has two quite different types of material to blend together and begin shaping the sermon.

Selecting an Approach

This is the time to solidify the question, the assertion, and the invitation and set out the approach to the subject and the congregation. Will the sermon argue its case deductively, inductively, or in some combination of the two? Will the major ideas be arranged chronologically, topically, causally, or in some other pattern?

The Second Sunday in Epiphany is the second or third Sunday in January. Both the Epiphany season and the beginning of the New Year are times for looking ahead. Theologically, the old covenant has served its purpose, and the law is fulfilled with the incarnation of the Lawgiver. Chronologically, the old year with its mix of bitter and sweet is gone, replaced by the new year that lies before us. January is often a depressing time because the holiday celebrations are over and winter seems like a permanent proposition. Also, there are many good church people for whom the coming of Christ has never brought a sense of joy or relief and for whom the gospel seems more bad news than good news. Given this blending of occasion, season, and mood, the sermon is intended as an encouraging and uplifting word.

John 2:1–11. The question, assertion, and invitation are as follows:

QUESTION: Can we be freed from the confining perspectives and conventions of the past?

ASSERTION: When Jesus comes, all is changed and everything becomes new.

INVITATION: Let us celebrate the newness of life that Jesus offers us.

Preaching on miracle accounts requires some care, for the surest way to kill the drama of the story is to approach it didactically, describing the background, arguing the case for the miraculous, and teaching the significance of the particular event. The trivia sheet contains a few sentences suggesting a narrative retelling of the story from the point of view of the bridegroom, the steward of the feast, or Mary. In the Gospels, a chronological pattern is almost always possible and could certainly be employed here. A problem-solution arrangement could be easily used: no wine (the problem) and the miracle (the solution). In the end, it was decided to develop the text and sermon topically in order to reveal the hidden complexities in a familiar passage and to address the issue of change in the believing community produced by the coming of Christ in the Epiphany season. It was further determined to tell the story of the text from the perspective of the guests at the wedding witnessing the events.

Structuring the Material

The study of the text will suggest many different organizing schemes. It is not unusual for the trivia sheet to contain half a dozen possible outlines. Looking over the text, exegesis notes, and sermon ideas, the preacher chooses the most suitable broad outline and begins the process of fitting mateiral into it. On a single page, the major headings are written in capitals and broadly spaced; then the preacher, working from both exegetical notes and trivia sheets, jots down under the appropriate headings brief indications of biblical material, support items, and specific applications that will fit in those sections.

John 2:1–11. The early reading of text and context noted the contrast between the ascetic and acerbic John the Baptist and the more human personality and style of Jesus. In the exegetical study, two further contrasts were observed: law and grace symbolized by the stone jars that were transformed from cleansing basins into wine vessels, and Jesus' turning from Mary to his mission for others. In a few minutes of refining, three major topics or aspects of change emerged:

> Prophet to Provider
> Cleansing Basins to Wine Vessels
> Mother to Others

These headings were printed on a sheet of paper, leaving one third of the page blank beneath each item. At this time only the body of the sermon is of concern; the introduction and conclusion are left until later. The raw sermon ideas are recorded under the main headings in no particular order, leaving a preliminary rough draft looking something like this:

I. Prophet to Provider (contrast of John the Baptist and Jesus)

TEXT: *JB:* a first-century Ralph Nader pointing out evils in society; a judgmental revivalist telling us that all we do is wrong; a medical expert telling us that everything we eat and drink causes cancer

Jesus: identified by the people with JB but goes to a party. The guests must have been expecting a wet blanket. Who would invite Isaiah, Jeremiah, Amos, or JB to a party? Probable reaction of guests when Jesus arrives: "Oh, no. The party's over."

ILLUS: Personal annoyance at being stereotyped as a minister

QUOTE: Karl Olsson's book *Come to the Party*

Jesus had a way of taking over parties: Mary and Martha's house, Matthew after his call. Maybe John isn't telling us about Jesus going to the party, but about the guests coming to Jesus' party

II. Cleansing Basins to Wine Vessels (law and grace)

TEXT: First-century Jewish wedding customs: week-long, entertainment, wine, dinners, ritual cleansing before coming

Wedding steward—provider, MC for entertainment, hired by groom's family

Stone jars—20–30 gallons (size of a large fish tank), hewn from stone for purity, placed for guests' convenience

STRESS: Shortcomings of the law, superiority of grace

ILLUS: Strange image of scrub sinks in hospital (where doctors scrub before surgery) filled with champagne punch

SOURCE: Sunday *NY Times Mag* article on change and depression

Biblical marriage imagery—Hebrew marriage symbolized God and Israel, New Testament, Christ and the church. Sacramental sense at a Jewish wedding; pious Jews confessed sins and fasted beforehand

III. Mother to Others

TEXT: Image of Mary as typical domineering mother telling adult son what to do. Mary concerned at party; thought Jesus might be helpful, probably not trying to be

boss, yet interjecting maternal relationship into Jesus' work
Jesus not disrespectful, but establishing necessary distance
Jesus' family given him by the Father—sometimes what is
closest to us can keep us from doing God's will
    ILLUS: Seminary student rejected by minister father
because he didn't approve of her seeking ordination
    STRESS: At some point, every person needs to put family
behind and strike out independently

N.B.: The lesson in these 3 topics isn't rejection but completion. Jesus doesn't repudiate JB but finishes his prophetic ministry. The wine of grace is the fulfillment of the water of the law.
Jesus doesn't reject his mother but goes beyond her to others.

Gathering Support Data

The raw material of the sermon has been placed in three
categories, producing a rough outline. This structure may or
may not bear close resemblance to the sermon as preached, but
it does give us an overview of the major framework and content.
The three headings serve as anchors, and we can pursue illustrations, quotations, and images in various sources and be able to
judge whether each item will, in fact, fit into the sermon.

At this point, the *New York Times* article would be reread,
as would Karl Olsson's *Come to the Party* and a pastoral counseling journal or book, consulted for what it can provide on faith
and change. The index of Bartlett's *Familiar Quotations* might
be scanned as well.

Composing the Outline

The Conclusion

Having gathered and placed in categories all the data to be
included in the sermon, the process of refinement that will result
in a finished outline begins. The work begins with the conclusion, the preacher asking, "What is the congregation being invited to believe, do, or experience as a result of the sermon?"

Having determined the invitation, the process is one of working backward through the body to the introduction so the message is a coherent whole building to the conclusion.

John 2:1–11. The conclusion will be brief, only a few sentences in length. As the theme of the sermon following the lesson is change after the arrival of Jesus at the party, the note struck is an invitation to celebrate the coming of Christ.

The Body

The major headings are reexamined and phrased in final form. Then each section is revised with the material under the headings set down in order. Some editing is inevitably done with items shifted from one section to another or eliminated altogether as not being appropriate or to fit the constraints of time. The body is restructured from beginning to end in clear outline form.

John 2:1–11. Although the three-heading format is retained, the first two topics are revised. Because the conclusion will be an invitation to the party, heading I is changed from "Prophet to Provider" to "Prophet to Partygoer." The sermon will not stress Jesus' miracle of providing wine so much as his presence at the feast. The incongruous image of a hospital scrub sink filled with champagne punch noted in the second section becomes the heading replacing the Johannine language of the text: "Cleansing Basins to Wine Vessels" gives way to "Scrub Sink to Punch Bowl." As events in the text will be related from the perspective of the party guests, the imagery is developed accordingly.

The Introduction

Despite (or, better, because of) its importance in establishing the sermon and securing the interest of the congregation, the introduction is the final component to be prepared. There are practical reasons for working back to the beginning in this way. A good introduction sparks the interest of hearers, raises the issue being addressed, and leads into the body, or assertion, that answers the question. Until the invitation is firm and the assertion fully developed, it stands to reason that composition of the introduction is premature. There is actually a danger in arriving too soon at a determination of the beginning of the sermon. The preacher who begins preparation around a clever introductory story or attention-getting example often finds that the Scripture text and other sermonic material cannot be forced to fit the opening, and much valuable time is lost trying to effect an impossible mating of ideas. As ideas for introductions occur, it is wise to jot them down and forego a final determination until the conclusion and body are in place.

John 2:1–11. The introduction for this sermon was recorded on the trivia sheet as a possible illustration during the exegetical study. It is an item from memory, an interview on an innocuous television variety show in which the smiling host asked a small boy if he attended Sunday school. When the lad replied in the affirmative, the host inquired, "What are you learning?"

"Last week," came the reply, "our lesson was about when Jesus went to a wedding and made water into wine."

"And what do you learn from that story?" asked the host.

The boy thought for a moment, fidgeted, and answered, "If you're having a wedding, make sure Jesus is there."

The outline, in its final form, is then written as follows:

TEXT: John 2:1–11

TITLE: "Come to the Party"

INTRODUCTION: Small-boy interview on TV show

TRANSITION: Significance for Epiphany—celebrating the coming of Christ in the new covenant; everything becomes new

I. PROPHET TO PARTYGOER
   A. Expectations of wedding guests
     1. John the Baptist—the prophet
      First-century doomsayer in the tradition of

Ralph Nader

A revivalist

A medical expert

ILLUSTRATION: Recent dinner with a food chemist critical of whole menu

  2. Jesus—the partygoer

    a. Identified with John the Baptist

    b. Party guests probably dreaded his coming

  B. Expectations of people today

    1. Perception of Christians as joyless people

ILLUSTRATION: Frustration of ministers at being stereotyped as one-dimensional people

    2. Jesus came that the lives of his people might be full

TRANSITION: Passing of prophetic office. God once spoke directly to his people; he does so once again in the Incarnation

II. SCRUB SINKS TO PUNCH BOWLS

ILLUSTRATION: Imagery of hospital in which the scrub sinks with gleaming long faucet handles are filled with champagne punch

  A. The law observed—scrub sinks

    1. Stone basins and ceremonial washing

    2. The Jews were so concerned with the keeping of the law that they missed the fulfillment of it in Christ

  B. The law fulfilled—punch bowls

    1. Jesus changes not only the water but the basins too

    2. Jesus can take us beyond the drudgery of legalism to the joy of fulfillment and forgiveness

TRANSITION: The law may now pass, for the Lawgiver has come

III. MOTHER TO OTHERS

  A. Family pressure

    1. Mary interposed in Jesus' work

    2. Contemporary family interposition

ILLUSTRATION: Female seminarian continuing to prepare for ministry although rejected by pastor father opposed to women's ordination

  B. Obedient independence

    1. Jesus again doing his Father's work

    2. Our need to see family as all of humanity

CONCLUSION: Come to the party

Writing the Manuscript

In some churches the sermon is not ordinarily delivered from a manuscript and congregations are actually resistant to hearing a preacher who brings the sermon written or typed into the pulpit. This tradition must be respected, for nothing is gained if the mode of delivery precludes a fair hearing. Writing the message in its entirety is a valuable discipline, however, and pastors who will never or only rarely preach from a manuscript still benefit from the writing exercise. Setting the sermon down on paper so ingrains the message in the mind that many preachers find no need for either outline or manuscript when they stand to preach.

The process of drafting the sermon is similar to that of composing the outline. First the conclusion is written and set aside. Then the body is drafted section by section, giving attention to time allotment and proportion. When the major sections are complete, the important transitions between sections are written. Last, the introduction is composed and the draft of the sermon is complete.

For unknown reasons, there are preachers who write out everything but the transitions. The result is often a sermon that shows excellent internal integrity but lurches from topic to topic without a sense of flow. If the preacher is rushed and has only a limited time to write the sermon, the conclusion, transitions, and introduction should be written first. These components usually account for about 20 percent of the sermon's content, and they are the portions in which precise wording is the most critical.

In order to avoid sounding like a journal article and yet maintain good oral style, you should say the words of the sermon before they are put down on paper. It is therefore appropriate, that the preacher have a private place to work, where he or she can speak out loud without alarming parishioners or family members. A story, a transition, or a paragraph explaining the text can be recited in clear, simple style and then, when it sounds right, written. A tape recorder is helpful at this stage, with the pastor dictating, playing back, and writing down. The more one rehearses the sermon orally before drafting, the clearer the style will be, resulting in a manuscript that will require a minimum of revision.

While rates of speaking vary, a double-spaced page of typescript containing 250–280 words will generally represent two minutes of preaching time. A nine- or ten-page manuscript, therefore, will convert to an eighteen-to-twenty-minute sermon.

The sermon should be arranged so that it is easily read. Some preachers prefer standard paragraph form, while others indent and stagger lines in the manner employed by Peter Marshall. It is a mistake to type the sermon completely in capitals, on the grounds that upper-case letters are easier to read than lower-case. In practice, when everything is capitalized, the finished page is actually harder to read, for it becomes difficult to pick up the beginnings of sentences.

An appropriate target time for completing the sermon is Friday morning; this provides the better part of two days for review and adjustment. With underlining or the use of a felt-tip marker to highlight key words and phrases, the preacher in the pulpit can, at a glance, retrieve entire sentences and paragraphs, making a word-for-word reading unnecessary.

Building a Preaching Library

Seminarians and beginning pastors are traditionally concerned about books, and rightly so. A library is to the preacher what the tool chest is to the mechanic or laboratory equipment is to the chemist. Theological volumes should be chosen with care, not only because books are expensive to purchase but also because they are heavy and cumbersome to move and shelve. Over the course of a career, a minister will move several times. Each move means that books must be boxed, insured, transported, unpacked, and rearranged in new space. A library occupies a considerable area; the more books the pastor owns, the greater the shelf footage required.

It is prudent for those starting out in ministry to curb their book-buying appetites and learn to use a few books well rather than many infrequently. Seminary professors offer advice on wise purchases in their fields, and bibliographic guides are readily available. Strive for quality over quantity in the study. A theological education trains the pastor to use critical scholarly sources, and these should be acquired and used. As theological scholarship is evolutionary rather than revolutionary in nature, older critical works age well and remain useful for decades, even centuries. A not-too-distant cousin to the book of sermon illustrations is the homiletical commentary. Invariably carrying the words "pulpit," "preacher's," "homiletical," or "practical" in the title and reprinted for years on end, advertised in denominational magazines, and marketed as an aid to the busy pastor, these volumes look impressive on the shelf and sound terrible from the pulpit. With thirty or forty large red- or blue-jacketed books, these sets serve to provide an academic backdrop behind the pastor's desk and can also be used to block up the family car when doing a brake job, but such uses probably fail to justify the purchase price.

8

Delivering
the Finished Product

This book has been concerned primarily with sermon preparation. After an initial chapter defining the task, six chapters were devoted to the study and framing of the verbal message. Why now is only a single concluding chapter given to sermon delivery?

The proportions of this study should not be seen to imply that instruction in delivery is unimportant, for this is certainly not the case. It is appropriate, however, to see the space allotment in this volume as an indication of the relative significance of the two major spheres of preaching, content and delivery. Simply stated, if we are given a choice, skill in sermon preparation is to be preferred to skill in sermon delivery. If the sermon is flawed in content, no amount of vocal facility is going to make it right.

Although sermons are often printed and distributed in written form, it must be admitted that something is lost from the oral presentation. The script of *Hamlet* may be read, as may the score of *A German Requiem,* but neither Shakespeare nor Brahms wrote for readers sitting by the fire. Drama and music come to life in the theater and concert hall, and the same is true of preaching; it is in live delivery that the sermon has its being.

The function and importance of delivery may be understood in an analogy to the printed page. The sermon is a popular medium, the theological equivalent of a mass-circulation magazine. A lecture, by way of contrast, could be compared to an academic journal, with page after page of black print marching in parallel columns from top to bottom with no variation in format. Because the content is "academic" and "rational," the editors of a journal make little effort to appeal to the eye with variety in typeface, composition, or layout. A mass-circulation magazine is a different proposition. If a base of subscribers and newsstand buyers adequate to support the publication is to be secured, the magazine must have appeal beyond its content. Color, graphics, photographs, and creative space utilization are employed to make the product attractive to the eye as well as to the mind.

As with the popular magazine, the ultimate destination of the sermon is the mind. And as the magazine must first appeal to the eye to reach the mind, so the sermon must first clear the gate of the ear to arrive at the hearer's consciousness. There is at least a rough oral equivalency to many of the devices employed by editors in print media. The attention gained by a headline of large bold capital letters, for example, is akin to the preacher's raising the volume of the voice. Something especially important set in italics in print may be underscored by the preacher by lowering the voice almost to a whisper. Graphic devices such as charts and graphs have their vocal equivalent in the quotation. When reaching the end of one subject, the editor may leave a blank line or two before resuming the discourse with a new topic; the skilled speaker can pause for several seconds when changing emphasis. The color photograph as it appears in a glossy magazine has as its homiletical counterpart the illustration, an oral depiction that allows the mind's eye to see the point being argued.

The delivery of a classroom lecture or the reading of an academic paper often has little ear appeal. Such presentations are the oral counterparts of the journal article. When such delivery is heard from the pulpit, lay people react with something less than enthusiasm, and properly so. The sermon is not an academic treatise but a popular presentation and application of biblical truth. If people are to be motivated to biblical living as well as instructed in biblical verities, it is the preacher's task to deliver the message in a way that will motivate the hearers to action.

Coping with Nervousness

Beginning public speakers are almost always traumatized by the very thought of speaking before an audience. The problem of stage fright is an obstacle that must be cleared by those who will earn their livings speaking before audiences.

Nervousness usually manifests itself in jerky patterns of motion or gesture, irregular breathing, or a too-rapid rate of delivery. In extreme cases, a preacher may suffer a mental block and be unable to remember the sermon. Often students ask me what they can do to avoid the increasing emotional turmoil they feel as the moment for delivering the sermon nears and finally arrives. The answer I usually provide may not be very helpful—and definitely is not the word they want to hear. I tell them that to my knowledge the only sure cure for stage fright is embalming fluid. From the first sermon we deliver until we go to our reward, these anxieties will be always with us. This is as it should be, for when the pastor no longer experiences nervousness, preaching has become mechanistic and devoid of feeling.

Those who week after week endure attacks of shaky knees, sweaty palms, and queasy stomachs may find encouragement in two observations born of experience. The first is that much nervousness may be attributed to inadequate preparation, and the obvious antidote is thorough study. A well-prepared preacher is usually a confident preacher. The second word of comfort is that fear generally abates with experience. Occasionally there are difficult sermons that for whatever reasons exceed the customary anxiety quotient, but the week-by-week routine of preaching not only provides needed experience for the preacher but also deepens the pastoral relationship in the congregation. The result is a growing sense of ease in conducting worship and delivering the sermon.

The delivery of sermons has two concerns beyond the inner tranquillity of the preacher: the visual, including the appearance, mannerisms, and gestures of the preacher; and the vocal, which focuses on the preacher's use of the human voice.

Visual Image

Appearance

In whatever setting we find ourselves, our dress and grooming make a statement. A spate of recent books stemming largely from the rise of women up the corporate ladder gives advice on clothing choices for those who seek success in business. As pastors, our selection of Sunday morning attire should be determined not by personal ambition but by what will enhance the congregation's worship experience and hearing of the gospel. In most churches, the garb of the pastor is all but predetermined: higher church traditions expect clerical attire, including gown, surplice, and stole; lower church practice dictates civilian clothing like that worn by the worshiping congregation. Given the rich and wide variety of ecclesiastical traditions in which Christians worship, there is little reason to advance a case for right or wrong clerical attire. The issue is not so much what is worn but how and why it is appropriate.

The overriding concern is that the preacher's appearance not call attention to itself. That is, whatever is worn should suit both the church and the occasion. In arguing for the wearing of a pulpit gown over a clerical collar with the seasonal stole, the point can be made that the one who guides the people in worship ministers not in his or her own authority but as a servant of the church. The vestments become a uniform, an identifying mark of one taken from the congregation and ordained to a specific sacred task. In response to the argument that clerical attire serves to create a gap between clergy and laity, the point can be made that it is the setting apart of called and gifted people by the laying on of hands in ordination that establishes the separation, not the attire worn by the minister. The donning of appropriate vestments maintains the tradition of the church and affirms the calling of the pastor.

If clothing of personal choice is visible, it should be plain and conservatively styled. A striped shirt or patterned blouse under a robe is less appropriate than solid white. If a suit or dress is the preferred attire, it should be dark and plain. Accessories should be simple, with little or no jewelry worn. In one of those intriguing and irritating inconsistencies of human behavior, pastors who would never wear a violet stole in Advent or red at Pentecost will take to the pulpit wearing the colors of an academic hood. More than one pastor who has never worn a robe suddenly appears in the sanctuary on a fine June Sunday morning gowned and garlanded with a bright new honorary doctor of divinity hood bestowed by an alma mater at spring commencement. Politicians, philanthropists, business executives, and even entertainers regularly collect honorary degrees without using the titles or parading the colors. It might be wished that those ordained to service in the church would follow their wise example. The pulpit is the place to preach the message of Christ, not to parade the academic pedigree of the preacher. Attire that exalts the messenger inevitably calls humility into question and detracts from the message.

Pulpit Manner

How pastors comport themselves in worship duties is a matter of personal and traditional preference. Logistic factors, such as the design of the sanctuary, are important as well: an open chancel invites movement, while an elevated, enclosed central pulpit confines the action to a small area. Movement should be purposeful and, like appearance, not call attention to itself. When the minister's demeanor suggests tension or self-consciousness, the congregation catches the spirit of discomfort, and the flow of communication is impaired.

An important aspect of ministerial presence in the sanctuary that rarely draws comment is the image projected by the pastor when he or she is not leading or preaching. The model of the pastor singing hymns, joining in the prayers and responses, and giving undivided attention to the choir and lay leaders is extremely important. When the minister refers to the order of service before the sermon as the "preliminaries," reviews the sermon during the hymn preceding, or pays no apparent heed to the choral anthem or reading of the lessons, church members may come to regard these elements as of little consequence. Such a spirit will inevitably spawn resentment in those who assist in the service, for they will come to see their efforts as little more than second-line acts warming up the congregation for the headliner in the pulpit.

Gesture

Elocution textbooks of a century ago defined and illustrated dozens of gestures and provided instructions on their proper use. To emphasize a critical point, the orator might push out the left foot, thrust the head forward, raise the right arm with fist clenched, extend the left hand toward the audience with the palm upward, and arch the eyebrows dramatically. Any speaker who could remember to perform all those moves and continue with the speech deserved to be elected president! We are fortunate that speech instruction in our day tends to advance a more natural style of public address.

Although there is no limit to the specific motions that may be employed in preaching, all gestures may be cataloged according to two types: *emphatic* and *descriptive.* An emphatic gesture underscores or reinforces a point, a kind of visual underlining employing a clenched fist, extended forefinger, or sharp downward arm movement. A descriptive gesture is a visual explanation: the use of both hands to show a spherical shape or the separation of the hands to indicate the length of a fish. Some descriptions are all but impossible to relate without gestures, as in the upward spiral of a circular staircase or the size of one's dog.

Gestures, like motion, should be purposeful. There are preachers who use many gestures and others who use few, and one style is not to be preferred over the other. Given cultural and traditional differences, we would expect the black Pentecostal pastor to be more animated than the white Anglican rector across town. No matter what the tradition, however, a wooden appearance with little or no motion to vary the image is generally dull, and constant movement is a distraction. With experience and the development of a personal style, preachers generally find an appropriate middle ground.

Vocal Presentation

A Unique Instrument

Electronic technology in the form of voiceprint recorders has discovered that no two human voices are exactly alike. As each fingerprint is unique, so each voice has its own signature. God has protected our individuality by creating each one of us quite different from anyone else on earth. Not only is uniqueness stamped on us by our backgrounds, experiences, physical attributes, and personalities, even the way we speak is different from the speech of any other human being.

The genius of preaching, as developed in chapter 1, is not only God speaking through his Word but God speaking through his messenger, as well. The singular note sounded by the individual preacher will burst forth not only from the unique person that the preacher is but also from the unique God-given voice the preacher has.

Every speaker must learn to work within the limits and potential of her or his own physical vocal equipment. Only a few preachers are blessed with a stained-glass voice—a booming trumpet that fills the greatest cathedral, charms the birds out of the trees, shatters crystal, reverses the tide, and defies contradiction. Most pastors have to work to get the maximum good from what they have been given. Understanding the mechanics of speaking and how we use our voices will assist in this development.

The Process of Human Speech

As human beings we are separated from the animals not so much by physique (many primates share our body configuration), or even by intellect (dolphins have brain power that approaches our own), but by the capacity to develop and communicate with language. Because we have language, premeditated intelligent discourse is possible, and we have a power of socialization not shared by other species. Although chimpanzees have been taught to say a few words, and other animals can understand simple commands, God has endowed only humanity with speech.

The foundation of speech is a flow or column of air, taken into the lungs and forced upward through the trachea, where it is constricted and accelerated in speed. In the trachea are vocal folds, often misnamed vocal cords, which vibrate much as a reed, producing raw sound. This raw sound passes into the mouth, where it is formed into intelligible sound (usually words) by the articulators: the tongue, teeth, gums, hard and soft palates, and lips. The resonating cavities in the mouth, sinuses, and chest amplify the sound and give it a distinctive quality or timbre.

As strange as it may seem, most beginning singers, speakers, and actors need to be taught how to breathe correctly. Proper inhalation begins with a downward movement of the diaphragm, a large muscle that bisects the body below the lungs. As the volume of the chest cavity is increased, air rushes in through the nose and mouth to fill the vacuum. When the diaphragm is relaxed, the air is expelled or exhaled up out of the lungs and through the trachea. While we breathe naturally from the diaphragm during sleep or at times of exertion, the tendency of most people when speaking is to breathe from the upper body or chest. Breathing from the chest area allows only a partial expansion of the lungs, resulting in a loss of breath control. Upper body breathing also requires a tightening of muscles that actually constricts the voice.

An excellent simple exercise may be performed to assist in diaphragmatic breathing. Stand sideways before a full-length mirror and place one hand on the abdomen. Push out against the hand with the stomach muscles while inhaling. Then push in with the hand and expel the air. Then do several repetitions with the hands at the sides. A warning is in order: the diaphragm is a muscle, and when exercised after underuse it will be as sore as other body muscles after an unaccustomed workout. The preacher who practices and masters diaphragmatic breathing, however, will speak with great breath control and less strain on the vocal apparatus.

Care of the Voice

Proper breathing is the most important safeguard for the protection of the voice while actually speaking. There are also precautions that may be observed before and after preaching that will keep the vocal equipment in good working order.

Aerobic exercise benefits the entire body, including the voice. Jogging, running, swimming, bicycling, or any other activity that leaves the participant winded increases lung power. An increased breathing capacity for the speaker or singer means improved breath control, greater stamina, and smoother delivery. The antithesis of aerobic exercise is smoking. The minister who smokes destroys lung capacity and function while running a great risk of contracting emphysema, heart disease, or cancer of the lungs, throat, or mouth. For the person whose profession demands a strong voice, the decision to smoke is a poor one indeed.

Just as those arising early to go deep-sea fishing eat different-size breakfasts depending on the strength of their stomachs, those who enter the pulpit show a similar variety in diet. One pastor will work better after a large breakfast, while a colleague will eat little if anything. This is a matter of metabolism, nervousness, and personal preference. One rule that should be observed is not drinking milk or eating milk products for at least two hours before speaking. Milk tends to leave a coating on the mucous linings in the mouth and throat which is difficult to clear. The flow of saliva becomes impaired, and an uncomfortable dry or cotton mouth is often the result. Drinking a glass of water shortly before worship helps maintain the saliva flow.

In leading worship and preaching, the pastor consumes as much energy as a laborer working an eight-hour shift. The body burns calories at a greatly accelerated rate when adrenaline courses through the bloodstream. When there are two sermons to be preached on a Sunday (or even three), or when there is a teaching responsibility in addition to worship, the pastor has put in more than a full day's work. After pronouncing the benediction, there is a need for some caution. The usual custom of greeting parishioners at the door appears innocent enough, except that in a cold climate the minister goes from a warm sanctuary with an even warmer elevated chancel perspiring under a heavy robe and stands in a drafty outer doorway where the temperature may be sixty or more degrees colder and shakes hands with dozens of people, of whom several are certainly carrying cold and flu germs. (A similar hazardous temperature variation occurs in air-conditioned churches in warm weather.) The simple solution is to perform the greeting ritual inside, well away from an open door.

Use of the Voice

As with the instruments that make up an orchestra, each human voice has its own sound and quality and may be played with greatly varying degrees of skill. An audience will not long tolerate listening to the same note played over and over again. It is the variety of sounds and rhythms that makes music interesting and appealing. The way to effective vocal presentation from the pulpit is making use of the range of the human voice. We achieve variety in vocal quality by varying rate, volume, and pitch.

Rate. The usual pace of discourse in public speaking ranges from 120 to 150 words a minute. The human ear is able to hear and differentiate about 400 words a minute, but we can tolerate such a rush only briefly. The maximum speed for any kind of sustained listening seems to be approximately 185 words per minute, but even this rate becomes fatiguing before long.

There are people with a naturally rapid rate of speech who must concentrate on slowing their delivery when standing before an audience. A significant cultural factor is operative here as well. Mediterranean and Latin American people, for example, tend to talk faster than northern Europeans. Often a delivery that is too rapid is the consequence of stage fright; the preacher tries to burn off nervous energy with a rush of words and may even be unaware of speaking quickly. Speech that is too fast not only is difficult for the listener to absorb and comprehend but causes problems for the speaker as well. Articulation is difficult when the delivery is rushed, and expression suffers as the voice flattens out at a single pitch.

Conversely, while there are fewer preachers whose rate is too slow, hesitant or halting delivery carries its own set of problems. We can think faster than we can listen, and if the preacher fails to keep the sermon moving, the congregation may mentally bail out. Also, slow delivery is sometimes perceived, correctly or incorrectly, as a lack of preparation or confidence on the part of the preacher.

Volume. The level of loudness necessary to carry a message depends on a host of factors: the size of the congregation, the design of the sanctuary, the tradition of the church, and the use or nonuse of a public-address system. Professional announcers and performers on radio and television have made us conscious of precise diction and articulation and have created a preference for a speaking style that is more restrained than that of earlier generations. The oratorical mode of address practiced of necessity before the invention of the microphone sounds artificial and overblown to ears conditioned first by such radio pioneers as Arthur Godfrey, Lowell Thomas, and Franklin Roosevelt and later by such television personalities as Walter Cronkite, Barbara Walters, Jane Pauley, Ted Koppel, and Bryant Gumbel.

It seems that even the smallest sanctuaries today come complete with loudspeakers—and this is a mixed blessing. There may be some benefit in assisting the projection of the pastor's voice, but microphones are tricky instruments to use well. Flexibility and intimacy are often sacrificed, and unless a portable microphone is employed, the preacher is chained to the pulpit. When there is proper projection and articulation by those speaking, it is a rare church building that actually requires an electronic sound system. An aggravation to pastors that without doubt has its origins in the congregations in Jerusalem, Rome, Corinth, and the seven churches of Revelation is that people tend to seat themselves in proximity to the pulpit according to their ability to hear. That is, those with ears like foxes sit in the front pews, while those suffering a hearing loss often take the rearmost seats. The cry for a public-address system in the sanctuary invariably comes from the back pews, and the suggestion that perhaps those who experience difficulty in hearing might take seats closer to the front is greeted as a new form of heresy. Church architects and decorators, who should know better, compound the problem by designing worship spaces with poor acoustics and then filling them with sound-deadening material —carpets, pew cushions, draperies, and porous ceiling tile. The result is a building in which congregational and choral singing has little vitality, and electronic equipment that would do justice to the Astrodome must be installed for the preacher to be heard. When a parish faces a building or remodeling program, among the first persons consulted should be an acoustical engineer.

Pitch. As a general rule, a lower speaking voice is more pleasing to the ear than a higher pitched or strident one. Until recently few women's voices were heard on the airwaves, as it was assumed that a broadcasting voice, to carry authority, had to be male and baritone. (If the truth were told, resistance to women as pastors probably springs more from this assumption than from any theological or biblical considerations.) Although the pitch of our voices is largely determined at birth, those whose voices tend toward the higher register can assist nature. Breathing from the diaphragm and relaxing the upper body muscles and throat will result in a lower tone. Also, as the voice is much like a muscle whose flexibility and strength increase with exercise, singing the alto or bass line of hymns rather than the melody will deepen the range.

Variation in tone and inflection is essential if an audience is going to listen to a speaker for any length of time. Those who fail to use the range of their voices to vary their inflection pattern are usually unaware of how their voices are perceived by listeners. It then becomes a matter of practice and concentration for the speaker to change pitch during delivery. A few people are unable to distinguish musical tones—at one time such people were called tone-deaf, although speech and hearing specialists now contend that there is no such malady as tone-deafness and diagnose the problem as a "lazy ear." Whatever the label, some people, preachers among them, need to be taught to hear differences in pitch. Until this ability is attained, the monotone voice will be a chronic and serious detriment to capturing and maintaining the interest of the congregation.

Maintaining Skill

As is true in any activity involving skill, it is distressingly easy to acquire bad habits in sermon delivery. Just as athletes develop faults that affect performance and result in slumps, preachers can develop problems in pulpit delivery through neglect or carelessness. Unless the preacher has a method of checking herself or himself, these faults may persist, to the detriment of the church's preaching ministry. If there is a trained speech professional available for consultation, and if the pastor can accept criticism and coaching without becoming defensive, periodic review sessions with such a person can be invaluable. Usually the preacher will have to be a self-critic. Although most of us do not spend our precious spare time listening to old sermon tapes, an occasional critical review will go a long way toward eliminating faults in delivery. Sitting down with every Sunday's sermon may be too much of a burden; once a month is probably all that is needed to pick up on such faults as poor diction, dropping the volume at the ends of sentences, inadequate expression, or problems with the rate of speaking. If video-recording capacity is available and can be set up without disrupting worship, the visual image can be checked along with the oral presentation.

Although preachers are hardly immune to criticism by parishioners, the pastor is rarely the subject of a thorough, positive evaluation in the church. Opportunities for evaluation and development are available through study centers, specialized conferences, and continuing-education programs. For far too many members of the clergy, the final and only systematic evaluation of their preaching occurs in seminary. Such instruction is not meant to last a lifetime. If tools are to be sharpened, gifts developed, and skills maintained, it is the preacher's responsibility to seek out and participate in programs designed to strengthen the ministry of the Word.

Epilogue

The most satisfying activities in life are those we can never completely master. At lunch not long ago a faculty colleague expressed his frustration over golf. "I've been playing for five years," he said. "Last season I thought I had the game licked, but this year my swing has gone to pieces. Now I'm right back where I started." As one who has struggled with the game for thirty years with never a claim of having mastered it, I listened with amusement to my colleague's lament.

Golf is a fiendishly difficult game to play well. Having been preaching for twenty years, I can testify that preparing and delivering sermons is no less difficult. It is, in fact, one of those activities that is satisfying and frustrating at the same time—like golf, oil painting, bridge, cabinetmaking, and French cooking—because the practitioner can work at it for a lifetime and never master it. We can take satisfaction in the sense of creativity and accomplishment that preaching brings, but we become frustrated in the knowledge that with more time, wisdom, patience, experience, or whatever we could do it better.

God does not expect us to be perfect preachers, only dedicated ones. In his wisdom, God has bestowed on us varying measures of creativity, exegetical and research abilities, language skills, and vocal fluency. It is our responsibility to be good stewards of these gifts, that the world may learn about the love of Christ and the church may be strengthened through the preaching of the Word.

For Further Reading

Chapter 1: Defining the Task

Barth, Karl. *Prayer and Preaching.* SCM Press, 1964.

Brooks, Phillips. *Lectures on Preaching.* Richard D. Dickenson, 1881.

Fisher, Wallace E. *Who Dares to Preach? The Challenge of Biblical Preaching.* Augsburg Publishing House, 1979.

Ford, D. W. Cleverly. *The Ministry of the Word.* Wm. B. Eerdmans Publishing Co., 1979.

Jabusch, Willard. *The Person in the Pulpit: Preaching as Caring.* Abingdon Press, 1980.

Read, David H. C. *Sent from God: The Enduring Power and Mystery of Preaching.* Abingdon Press, 1973.

Sweazey, George. *Preaching the Good News.* Prentice-Hall, 1976.

Van Der Geest, Hans. *Presence in the Pulpit: The Impact of Personality in Preaching.* John Knox Press, 1981.

Chapter 2: Determining the Subject

Abbey, Merrill R. *Communication in Pulpit and Parish.* Westminster Press, 1973.

Engel, James F. *Contemporary Christian Communications: Its Theory and Practice.* Thomas Nelson, 1979.

Kraft, Charles H. *Communication Theory for Christian Witness.* Abingdon Press, 1983.

Reid, Clyde H. *The Empty Pulpit: A Study in Preaching as Communication.* Harper & Row, 1967.

Chapter 3: Planning a Preaching Schedule

Abbey, Merrill R. *The Shape of the Gospel: Interpreting the Bible Through the Christian Year.* Abingdon Press, 1970.

Asquith, Glenn H. *Preaching According to Plan.* Judson Press, 1968.

Bass, George. *The Song and Story.* CSS Publications, 1984.

Fuller, Reginald H. *Preaching the New Lectionary: The Word of God for the Church Today.* Liturgical Press, 1974.

Skudlarek, William. *The Word in Worship: Preaching in a Liturgical Context.* Abingdon Press, 1981.

Chapter 4: Organizing the Discourse

Crum, Milton. *Manual on Preaching: A New Process of Sermon Development.* Judson Press, 1977.

Davis, H. Grady. *Design for Preaching.* Fortress Press, 1958.

Lowry, Eugene L. *The Homiletical Plot: The Sermon as Narrative Art Form.* John Knox Press, 1980.

Massey, James Earl. *Designing the Sermon: Order and Movement in Preaching.* Abingdon Press, 1980.

Chapter 5: Making the Sermon Memorable

Achtemeier, Elizabeth. *Preaching as Theology and Art.* Abingdon Press, 1984.

Buechner, Frederick. *Telling the Truth: The Gospel as Tragedy, Comedy, and Fairy Tale.* Harper & Row, 1977.

Steimle, Edmund A., Morris J. Niedenthal, and Charles L. Rice. *Preaching the Story.* Fortress Press, 1980.

Troeger, Thomas H. *Creating Fresh Images for Preaching: New Rungs for Jacob's Ladder.* Judson Press, 1982.

Chapter 6: Making the Meaning Clear

Achtemeier, Elizabeth. *Creative Preaching: Finding the Words.* Abingdon Press, 1980.

Ebeling, Gerhard. *Introduction to a Theological Theory of Language.* Tr. by R.A. Wilson. Fortress Press, 1973.

Fant, Clyde E. *Preaching for Today.* Harper & Row, 1977.

Chapter 7: Preparing the Sermon

Best, Ernest. *From Text to Sermon: Responsible Use of the New Testament in Preaching.* John Knox Press, 1978.

Broadus, John A. *On the Preparation and Delivery of Sermons,* 4th ed. Harper & Row, 1978.

Cox, James W. *A Guide to Biblical Preaching.* Abingdon Press, 1976.

Fee, Gordon D. *New Testament Exegesis: A Handbook for Students and Pastors.* Westminster Press, 1983.

Gowan, Donald E. *Reclaiming the Old Testament for the Christian Pulpit.* John Knox Press, 1980.

Marshall, Peter. *Mr. Jones, Meet the Master.* Fleming H. Revell Co., 1949.

Scholer, David M. *A Basic Bibliographic Guide for New Testament Exegesis.* Wm. B. Eerdmans Publishing Co., 1973.

Stuart, Douglas. *Old Testament Exegesis: A Primer for Students and Pastors.* Rev. and enlarged ed. Westminster Press, 1984.

Wardlaw, Don M., ed. *Preaching Biblically: Creating Sermons in the Shape of Scripture.* Westminster Press, 1983.

Chapter 8: Delivering the Finished Product

Bartow, Charles L. *The Preaching Moment: A Guide to Sermon Delivery.* Abingdon Press, 1980.